P9-EED-233

HOW TO FORM YOUR OWN INDIANA CORPORATION *BEFORE THE INC. DRIES!* with Disk

A Step-by-Step Guide, With Forms

by Phillip G. Williams, Ph.D.

Small Business Incorporation Series
Volume 4

second, revised edition

The P. Gaines Co.

PO Box 2253, Oak Park, Illinois 60303
Telephone (708) 524-9033

Copyright © 1997 by Phillip G. Williams

All rights reserved. No part of this book may be reproduced or transmitted in any form or by any means, electronic or mechanical, including photocopying, recording or by any information storage or retrieval system without written permission from the author, except for the inclusion of brief quotations in a review.

Since laws are subject to differing interpretations, neither the publisher nor the author offers any guarantees concerning the information contained in this publication or the use to which it is put. Although this publication is designed to provide accurate and authoritative information concerning incorporation in the state of Indiana, it is sold with the understanding that neither the author nor the publisher is engaged in rendering legal or other professional advice. If legal or other expert assistance is required, the services of a competent professional should be sought. *Adapted from a Declaration of Principles jointly adopted by a Committee of the American Bar Association and a Committee of Publishers.*

Library of Congress Cataloging in Publication Data

Williams, Phil, 1946-
    How to form your own Indiana corporation before the inc. dries!
with disk : a step-by-step guide, with forms / by Phillip G.
Williams. -- 2nd, rev. ed.
      p.   cm. -- (Small business incorporation series : v. 4)
    Includes index.
    ISBN 0-936284-19-6 (pbk. : alk. paper)
    1. Incorporation--Indiana.   2. Corporation law--Indiana.
I. Title.   II. Series.
KF13213.5.Z9W55   1997
346.772'06622--dc21   97-12994
                                           CIP

Cover design by **BENSEN STUDIOS,** Arlington Heights, Illinois

Software by **BIT CONSULTING,** Westmont, Illinois

Manufactured in the United States of America

Copyright is not claimed in any forms reprinted in this book which were obtained from official state of Indiana sources.

Table of Contents

Chapter 7. THE INDIANA NOT FOR PROFIT CORPORATION   78

Chapter 8. THE S CORPORATION   82

INTRODUCTION

If you are thinking of starting your own small business or have already done so, you may find yourself perplexed by the large number of laws governing your business activities. At one time, doing business in the United States was a much simpler affair. Most business activity consisted of small manufacturers and merchants offering their wares and services on a local or regional basis.

Today, the current trend is toward economic concentration in the hands of a small number of multinational corporations, who own everything from breakfast cereal firms to computer manufacturers.

We are also experiencing, on the other hand, a rediscovery of the individual entrepreneur, who has become a new kind of folk hero. Even large corporations at present are trying to tap into the strengths of entrepreneurial thinking. Some have designated individuals or even whole departments to work independently from the rest of the company in quest of more creative approaches to their business problems.

While some of the most astute large corporations are promoting entrepreneurial values as a part of their own structure, many entrepreneurs find themselves in need of following the opposite path. They stand to gain from learning the techniques of business that major corporations practice. Incorporation itself is one such practice that many small businesses are learning to profitably adapt to their own purposes.

We may wistfully recall the past and may even work for a reduction in our increasingly unwieldy business and tax regulations, but we cannot completely turn back the clock. With greater complexity and sophistication of techniques here to stay, many small businesses today wish to take advantage of the corporate form of operation.

A number of individuals as well as businesses can benefit from organizing their own corporation. Persons in administrative and consulting positions can often profitably quit their present jobs, form their own corporate firms, and sell their services back to their employers, to the advantage of both parties. Salespeople, writers, artists, and designers will, in many cases, stand to gain from incorporating, as will many others planning to start or already running their own businesses, whether it be a catering service or a construction firm. Professionals such as engineers, architects, dentists, nurses and other health professionals may profit from incorporating their practices as well.

Some of the advantages of incorporation include limited liability, greater financial flexibility, a low corporate income tax rate for retained earnings, and a host of tax-free benefits, such as tax-free life insurance, a plan that pays medical, dental, and drug costs and health insurance coverage, a tax-deductible salary-continuation and disability plan, a tuition reimbursement plan, free legal services, and corporate stock dividends that are 70 percent tax free.

The present book, designed to clarify the important business area of incorporation, is written specifically for Indiana individuals and businesses, providing a thorough discussion of the advantages and disadvantages of incorporation, tax angles, employee benefits, and a blueprint for setting up your own Indiana corporation.

In the back of this book, we provide all the forms necessary to organize an Indiana corporation. For ease of use, this new edition of the book also supplies all the incorporation forms on a personal computer disk, in the vinyl pocket affixed to the inside back cover.

Chapter 5 covers the procedure for forming a profit corporation, while Chapter 7 deals with the not for profit corporation. If you wish to form an Indiana Professional Corporation as a doctor, veterinarian, dentist, certified public accountant, psychologist, engineer, architect, or other licensed professional, you will find this type of corporation explained in Chapter 6.

If you prefer to do your own incorporation without a lawyer, you are entitled to do so, since you are not required by Indiana law to use an attorney to incorporate your business. Since the average attorney fee for an incorporation runs from $400 to $2,500, you will save money by incorporating yourself. On the other hand, if you already have a prospering business and little time to concern yourself with the details of incorporating, you can find a competent attorney skilled in this area through the local chapter of the American Bar Association.

If you do prefer to use the services of a lawyer to handle your incorporation, the information provided herein will help you ask the right questions of your attorney and make the most informed decisions. If you decide to fill out and file your own incorporation papers, we recommend having a lawyer review them, since even simple incorporations may have complications. You will still save money by following this procedure, since the charge for this service at an hourly rate (approximately $100 to $125) will be substantially less than the full incorporation fee.

If there are unusual aspects to your incorporation which are not treated in the following discussion, we also advise legal consultation prior to filing the Articles of Incorporation.

Chapter 1. FOUR FORMS OF BUSINESS OWNERSHIP

Until recently, the federal and state governments of the United States and their agents such as the IRS have recognized three legal forms of business ownership: the sole proprietorship, the partnership, and the corporation. All fifty states have recently adopted yet a fourth form of business operation, called the limited liability company.[1] While this book is primarily concerned with the category of the corporation, it is important to examine the other three by way of comparison. Each has distinct advantages and disadvantages.

Sole Proprietorship

If you operate your own business and have not incorporated or entered into a partnership agreement, you are automatically classified as a sole proprietor. In other words, a sole proprietor is one person engaged in a business for profit. The chief advantage of this form of operation is its informality. You can start up or terminate your business whenever you feel like it. The state or federal government cannot prevent you from starting this type of business, so long as it is not illegal. The sole proprietor can also freely mix personal and business finances, lumping all the money into one bank account or handling it however he or she pleases. Of course, the sole proprietor, like all business owners, has to pay taxes, so she must apply for a state sales tax number, keep records, file state and federal tax returns and follow all other procedures required by law. But as the least regulated of the four forms of business ownership, the sole proprietorship does not require permission from the state for its formation, operation, and dissolution.

---

1   While offering the advantage of limited liability, like a corporation, the limited liability company is structured taxwise like a partnership and sometimes requires a minimum of two persons to form. In 1993, Indiana put into effect a law authorizing this type of business entity in the state. The highlights of the provisions of that law are discussed in this chapter in the section on the "Limited Liability Company."

Furthermore, the sole proprietor may transfer the inventory of his business to personal use. In the case of the corner grocery store, the owner may simply choose to eat what he does not sell. If the store owner wants to take a chicken from his meat case or a cantaloupe from his fruit stand, he is free to do so.[2] If an employee of a corporation followed the same procedure, however, he would be guilty of theft.

The major disadvantage of the sole proprietorship is that the owner is personally liable for all the debts of the business and for any injuries caused to or by its employees acting in a business capacity. If your warehouse clerk drops a 50-gallon drum on his own head or on the head of one of your customers, for example, then you are personally responsible for the damages.[3] Therefore, as sole proprietor, not just your business assets are "at risk." If you owe creditors more than your business is worth or if a legal suit against you awards the plaintiff an amount in excess of your business assets, your personal assets as well—your bank account, your car, your home, your Persian rugs—may all be legally attached, and your salary garnisheed if you have other employment as well.[4] Your liability as a sole proprietor is limited only by the totality of all your possessions, personal as well as business.

Realistically speaking, many small businesses have no choice but to start existence as a sole proprietorship if the owner does not have sufficient time and resources to deal with the greater complexity entailed by the corporate form of operation. If the enterprise prospers, however, incorporation will become, in time, an increasingly attractive option.

Expert Advice on Sole Proprietorships and Accounting

An excellent book on starting and running a sole proprietorship is **Small Time Operator: How to Start Your Own Business, Keep Your Books, Pay Your Taxes, and Stay Out of Trouble!** *by Bernard Kamoroff, C.P.A. This book also includes a thorough treatment of accounting practices for the small business (whether incorporated or unincorporated) and contains enough actual ledger sheets and worksheets to last for a full year. This publication can be ordered from The P. Gaines Co. See the order form in the back of this book.*

---

2   It should be noted, however, that even the sole proprietor is required, for tax purposes, to keep a record of inventory adopted for personal use. This information is needed in completing the 1040 Schedule C form.

3   Insurance is one means of protection, although it is often an expensive way to limit personal liability. It may also be virtually impossible for the small business person to obtain at affordable rates. While corporations as well as sole proprietors generally carry insurance, if they can get it, the corporate form itself is a valuable protection against unlimited liability (with the exception of professional service corporations—see Chapter 6).

4   Every state has laws which exempt certain personal possessions from attachment to satisfy debts, so a creditor cannot literally take the clothes off your back. Chapter 7 debtors faced with liquidation of their assets have exemptions of $15,000 on their home ($30,000 for married couples), $2,400 on their car, and, under federal law, $1,500 on any implements, professional books, or trade tools.

Partnership

A partnership is a business for profit which is owned by two or more individuals. Partnerships resemble sole proprietorships, with special allowances demanded by the fact of more than one owner. Thus, the same advantages which the sole proprietor enjoys apply to the partnership as well, the lack of formal requirements being the chief benefit. There exist no special procedures for establishing a partnership; a simple verbal agreement is sufficient, although a written agreement in the event of future disagreements among partners is highly advisable.

Termination of the partnership is automatic upon the death, disability, or withdrawal of one of the partners (unless otherwise agreed). Another important advantage of the partnership is that it provides a framework for individuals to pool their resources, including money, skills, and ideas. In a partnership, the sum is often greater than the parts, since it permits persons acting together to achieve goals that none could attain individually.

The federal government's Uniform Partnership Act defines a partnership as "an association of two or more persons as co-owners of a business for profit." This act regulates the activities of partnerships in every state. It stipulates that the partners share equally in the profits and the losses, unless otherwise agreed. In a partnership, each partner owes the partnership a fiduciary duty to put the business interests of the partnership first. If partnership business is being siphoned off by one of the partners for his own use without the knowledge and consent of the other partners, that particular partner is guilty of defrauding the partnership and may be sued by the other principals.

As in the case of the sole proprietor, the partnership must follow all procedures, keep all records, and remit all forms and payments required by the state and federal taxing authorities. The partnership itself is not a taxable entity, however. The partnership annually reports its income to the IRS on an informational return (Form 1065), and the individual partners include their share of the profits on their personal 1040 tax returns. Thus a partnership determines its income and pays taxes in basically the same way as an individual sole proprietor.

Like the sole proprietor also, the chief disadvantage of the partnership is the personal liability of each partner for the debts of the partnership. All partners in a business are individually liable for all acts of the business. If your partner(s) is (are) unscrupulous or unwise, you stand to lose a great deal more than your initial investment.

In summary, the risks of partnerships are extensive, since partners have unlimited liability for all actions or omissions of the partnership or its individual partners, employees, or others acting in its name and behalf. Another disadvantage: When the assets of the partners are disproportionate and you are the partner with much greater assets, you stand to forfeit more in the event that partnership assets are inadequate to satisfy creditors' claims. In such an eventuality, your house may be attached and liquidated to pay business debts, whereas your undercapitalized partner may lose only her truck! Another disadvantage of the partnership is that each individual partner's profits are taxed in the year of receipt, whereas the corporate structure offers greater financial flexibility, often allowing you to spread profits over a number of years and thus reduce the tax bite.

Finally, under the Uniform Partnership Act there exists a special type of partnership called the "limited partnership," which combines aspects of a partnership and a corporation. A limited partnership has two classes of partners, defined as general and limited partners. The general partners assume the operation of the business. In a regular partnership, discussed above, all the partners are general partners. A limited partner, on the other hand, can invest in a partnership without involvement in its management and without the risk of personal liability. Unlike the general partner who has unlimited personal liability, the liability of the limited partner does not exceed the amount of his initial investment. Unlike a regular partnership, a limited partnership agreement, according to state law, can only be established in writing. Many types of real estate investment groups, for instance, will have both general partners who organize the venture and limited partners who invest in it. Interestingly enough, a marriage is considered a general partnership unless there is a written agreement in advance that it is to be treated as a limited partnership!

Let's Shake on It!

The Partnership Book *by Denis Clifford and Ralph Warner provides an excellent source of information about the nuts and bolts of setting up effective partnership agreements. It covers evaluation of partner assets, disputes, buy-outs, and the death of a partner. This publication can be ordered from The P. Gaines Co. Please see the order form in the back of this book for details.*

Important note

In general, corporations often work much better than partnerships for many types of businesses, for the reasons discussed above. There exists one type of business for which a partnership or a limited liability company structure may prove more advantageous in some circumstances, however, that of the professional firm. If you are a doctor or a lawyer or other kind of professional practitioner, you should explore with a skilled legal adviser whether the partnership or the limited liability company format offers particular advantages for you. Specifically in the areas of retirement payments and firm breakups, partnerships and LLCs may benefit the professional firm in ways not available to the corporation. See Chapter 6, "The Indiana Professional Corporation," for more discussion on this point.

Limited Liability Company

Contrary to the proverb, there *is* something new under the sun, the limited liability company. In 1991, only eight states recognized this form of business operation. Today, all fifty states, including Indiana, authorize the formation of LLCs. Combining features of a corporation and a partnership, the LLC allows its owners to enjoy the limited liability of the corporate structure while being taxed like a partnership. Thus, the income or loss of the LLC flows through to the individual owners, usually in proportion to their holdings, and appears on their personal income tax returns. Unlike many states, the LLC in Indiana does not require a minimum of two organizers, like a partnership. A single individual can form an LLC in Indiana.

What would be the advantage of forming an LLC instead of a corporation? In many situations, there would be no tax advantage, since an S corporation would give you the same tax structure as an LLC: the income or loss from the S corporation is divvied up among the individual owners just like a partnership or an LLC.

From an organizational standpoint, however, LLCs are much easier to form and administer than S corporations. A host of complex rules govern the establishment and maintenance of S corporations. Breaking one of these rules may result in the dissolution of the S corporation, with unfavorable tax consequences. In the case of LLCs, however, what you see is what you get. Once the LLC is formed, you don't have to petition the IRS for special tax status in order to be taxed like a partnership, as in the case of S corporations. You will automatically be taxed as a partnership. You cannot accidentally lose your partnership tax status, furthermore, by violating an obscure rule, as in the case of an S corporation.

As pointed out in the section on Partnerships above, professional firms, especially ones with numerous shareholders, might find the limited liability company structure more suited to their particular needs. The S corporation is limited to 75 shareholders; LLCs have no limitation on the number of members they may have. In addition, LLCs offer certain advantages to professional firms in the areas of retirement payouts and firm breakups which the S corporation does not offer. These are discussed further in Chapter 6, "The Indiana Professional Corporation."

There is another situation in which the formation of an LLC proves ideal, the area of joint ventures. Say, for instance, that a graphic designer and a printing company want to form a joint venture to sell a line of greeting cards. A partnership is one option, but an LLC has the obvious advantage of limiting liability. If the greeting card venture folded and creditors were owed substantial amounts, in the case of a general partnership the creditors could go after the assets of the individual partners. With an LLC, however, this is not the case. The personal assets of each of the members of the LLC would be off limits to creditors seeking to recover debts incurred by the LLC.

The Indiana Business Flexibility Act authorizing the formation of LLCs in the state went into effect on July 1, 1993. The LLC is particularly well suited for foreign

13

investment, venture capital, joint ventures, real estate, oil and gas and high technology transactions. We have suggested that professional firms, due to their unique organizational structure, may also be prime candidates for the LLC format. If you are involved in any ventures of this type, we recommend that you explore the advantages and disadvantages of this type of operation, as compared to the corporate form of doing business, with a competent legal adviser.

Given Indiana's allowance of the right of single individuals to form LLCs, LLCs also offer an attractive choice to sole proprietors in the state, allowing them to limit personal liability without involving the greater complexity of the corporate form of business organization. The fee in Indiana to set up an LLC is the same as that to organize a corporation, a filing fee of $90.

The P. Gaines Co. has recently launched a new series on the Limited Liability Company. Phone for details on when the volume for Indiana will be available.

Corporation

A corporation is a legal entity separate from its owner(s), manager(s), or operator(s). As a "legal person," it can conduct business, borrow and lend money, sue and be sued. Wanda Gold decides to incorporate her business and forms Wanda Gold Enterprises, Inc. Although Wanda is the sole owner and operator, her corporation in the eyes of the state has a distinct life of its own, separate from that of Wanda. It will be expected to pay taxes like a real person, it may enter into contracts, be named as a defendant or plaintiff in a lawsuit, acquire and hold property, and so on.

Unlike the sole proprietorship and the partnership, a corporation cannot be formed until you receive written approval from the state. The life of a corporation, its "birth," begins with the issuance of the Articles of Incorporation by the Secretary of State and ends with its voluntary or involuntary dissolution (as in the case of bankruptcy). The Indiana corporation statutes define the rules and procedures governing the formation, continuance, and termination of Illinois corporations.

Before we examine the mechanics of setting up your own corporation, however, let's take a closer look at the corporation as a form of business ownership.

Limited Liability

The majority of individuals forming Indiana corporations will enjoy the advantage of limiting personal liability by means of the corporate structure. Limiting liability, in fact, is traditionally one of the greatest incentives for incorporating a business. A corporate owner or director is not, in most cases, personally liable for the debts of the corporation. Therefore, if a lawsuit is brought against Wanda Gold Enterprises, Inc., only the assets of the corporation itself will be subject to collection, not the personal assets of Wanda herself (with certain important exceptions noted hereafter). This fact can be very comforting to someone just starting out in business.

From the standpoint of limiting liability, the corporate route may be worth it in terms of peace of mind alone. Not only will the owner and other stockholders not be liable for the debts of the corporation, over and above their investment in the corporation in the form of shares of stock. Risk ventures can also be undertaken with the same assurances—only the investment of the corporation will be "at risk," not personal property.

In the event of a financial disaster, corporations, like individuals, can go bankrupt. If your corporation suddenly owes creditors half a million dollars and the assets of the company are only $20 thousand, then the business could file for bankruptcy. Once the $20 thousand in assets was distributed to creditors, the bankruptcy court would declare the corporation to be legally dissolved and the remainder of the company debt would in effect be wiped out. You would then be free to start another corporation tomorrow with a new name, if you so desired.

This is not, of course, a recommendation that you form a corporation and amass huge debts and then cancel them out by filing for bankruptcy. Not only would such an intentional attempt to evade payment of bills be unethical, but most creditors would be unwilling to extend a large line of credit to you in the first place unless you were an established customer.

If it were apparent, moreover, that you intentionally formed a "thin" (undercapital-ized) corporation in order to avoid payment of debts, you would in all probability not escape personal liability. The courts in such cases in the past have tended to subject the shareholders of such corporations to personal liability. The point is that in the event of a major unforeseeable disaster—a lawsuit, large casualty loss, and so on—bankruptcy is a final "escape clause" for corporations which, unlike the sole proprietorship and the partnership, allows your personal assets to remain untouched.

The cases in which liability is *not* limited by the corporate structure generally fall into one of three categories: (1) taxes; (2) instances of gross negligence, fraud, mismanagement, or malpractice (especially in the case of professional service corporations); (3) personal assets pledged to secure a loan.

Regarding the matter of taxes, remember that the payment of taxes is the lifeblood of the state and federal governments. Strict laws and penalties safeguard this form of governmental livelihood. In this delicate area, even corporations are not exempt from sanctions, and, in some situations, an officer or employee of a corporation can be held personally liable for failure to withhold and pay taxes (if this is one of the defined duties of the employee's position, as treasurer, for instance).

Second, professional malfeasance may also trigger personal liability, as in the case of a director or officer who mismanages or takes advantage of the corporation.[5] This

---

5   We are not speaking here of honest errors of judgment but of gross negligence and downright intent to defraud.

type of misconduct most often involves plundering the corporate assets through actual theft or other instances of draining the company's financial reserves. Not giving the corporation the "right of first refusal" also falls under this category.

Other fraudulent acts, such as "doctoring" the corporate balance sheets, may result in personal liability as well. In such situations, the individual can be sued by the corporation and will be subject to personal financial liability for losses to the corporation. In addition to actual damages, punitive damages may also be assessed, and the party may be subject to criminal prosecution. Corporate directors of several large American banks have recently been convicted of this type of misconduct.

Under this same heading, it is important to realize that professional service corporations do not enjoy the same advantage of limited liability as other types of corporations.[6] A doctor or lawyer who has incorporated his practice, for example, will still be personally liable for any acts of professional misconduct, including malpractice, in his or her role as a practitioner of the profession. (Article 1.5 of Section 23 of the Indiana Code which covers the formation of professional corporations in the state does not remove the limited liability of the professional as a shareholder of the corporation, however.) This does not mean that incorporating does not offer other advantages to professionals. It sometimes does, so that individual professionals may find incorporating an advantage. See Chapter 6 for a detailed discussion of the Indiana Professional Service Corporation.

Third, creditors such as banks naturally wish to limit their risks as much as possible. An owner of a small corporation will often be asked to pledge personal assets as security for a loan. Obviously, the shield for personal assets which the corporate form provides in other situations will not work in this case.

In spite of these three important exceptions, the corporation does offer a limitation of liability not available to the sole proprietor or the partnership. In the event of legal damages you must pay, due to injury or loss to consumers caused by goods or services you manufacture or sell, your corporation will serve as a reliable umbrella, in most cases protecting your personal assets from attachment and liquidation. This advantage alone may be worth the

---

6   Professions authorized by Indiana law to form Professional Corporations include all licensed professions, such as architects, landscape architects, professional engineers, land surveyors, certified and public accountants and accounting practitioners, attorneys, real estate professionals, veterinarians, and the following health care professionals: chiropractors, dentists, nurses, optometrists, pharmacists, physical therapists, physicians, podiatrists, psychologists, and speech-language pathologists.

price of incorporation for most individuals.

The Corporation as a Tax Shelter

The corporation as a form of business ownership can save taxes in a number of ways not available to the sole proprietor or partnership, including corporate income tax rates lower than personal ones, corporate pension[7] and profit-sharing plans, corporate medical reimbursement plans, and other allowable business deductions.

The following examples show how federal income tax savings may be realized and income generated by incorporating, through a combination of lower corporate tax rates, benefit plans, and the structuring of the sale of a going business to the new corporation. The current graduated federal tax rate for corporations taxes the first $50,000 of income at 15 percent; income of $50,000 to $75,000 at a 25 percent rate; and income over $75,000 at a 34 percent[8] rate. (An additional 5 percent tax, up to $11,750, is imposed on corporate taxable income over $100,000. Corporations with taxable income of at least $335,000 pay a flat rate of 34 percent.) A corporation would pay $7,500 in federal taxes on $50,000 in income, for example, while a single individual would pay $11,134 at present in federal taxes on the same dollar amount.

Example 1

If Wanda Gold (a single individual) has $40,000 in taxable income, she would pay $8,087 in federal income tax, whereas Wanda Gold Enterprises, Inc. with the same taxable income would pay only $6,000 in federal taxes. Tax savings are only the tip of the iceberg, furthermore.

Consider the following situation. If Wanda Gold Enterprises, Inc. pays Wanda a salary of $25,000 for her services to the corporation, she would personally owe $3,887 in federal income tax under current rates. If her corporation showed a profit of $40,000 a year, Wanda's salary, assuming it is "reasonable," would be deductible from this amount as a necessary business expense, thus reducing to $15,000 the income taxable to the corporation.

If the corporation has a retirement plan, a profit-sharing plan, and a medical reimbursement plan,[9] however, the contributions of the corporation to each of these plans would also reduce dollar-for-dollar the corporation's taxable income. Each of these plans would provide a form of tax-free income to Wanda (while some of it would be direct income, some would be deferred income).

---

7 The 1982 tax act in effect eliminated much of the past favoritism of corporate retirement plans over Keogh plans for the self-employed sole proprietor, but the tax shelter advantages of all such plans remain immense. In one area, discussed in Chapter 4, the defined benefit corporate retirement plan still offers advantages over other plans for nonincorporated businesses.

8 The Clinton tax act of 1993 did create another, higher tax bracket for corporations (35 percent bracket), but this rate applies only to corporations with taxable income over $10 million.

9 An individual taxpayer can also deduct medical, dental, and prescription drug expenses, as well as medical insurance premiums, if he itemizes deductions, but only to the extent that such expenses, when lumped together, exceed 7.5 percent of adjusted gross income.

At the same time, the corporation could deduct the full amount of its contributions as ordinary expenses. If Wanda Gold Enterprises, Inc. pays out $9,000 during the year in medical reimbursements and pension and profit-sharing plan contributions for Wanda, for instance, it will show only $6,000 in taxable income ($900 in corporate federal tax will be owed, in other words). Taking into consideration Wanda's individual income tax of $3,887 paid on her salary and the corporate tax of $900, a total tax of $4,787 will be paid for the year.

Remembering that Wanda would have to pay $8,087 in taxes if she were on a straight salary of $40,000, a federal tax savings of $3,300 would be realized in this particular instance because of the corporate structure. Remember also that Wanda will have received $9,000 from the corporation in non-taxable benefits for that particular year as well, over and above the tax savings realized. Wanda's company could contribute up to $600 to her favorite charity, moreover, and deduct it from income as a business expense!

Example 2
You decide to incorporate a going business whose worth has been appraised at $220,000. By carefully structuring the sale of your sole proprietorship to your corporation, you can provide yourself a substantial, almost totally tax-free income for a number of years.

Here's how one such plan might work. Accept only a small portion of the total value of the business, say, $40,000, in stock from the newly formed corporation. For the remaining $180,000, take back a note from the corporation. (You are lending the corporation the additional $180,000 to buy the business, in other words.) If the term of the note is set for four years, you will receive principal and interest from the note over the next four years, with only the interest portion taxable (the rest is considered a non-taxable return of principal by the IRS). The major portion ($45,000 from return of principal each year) of the proceeds from the note will be tax-free.

The above examples illustrate some of the many tax-saving devices available to corporations. These strategies will be discussed further in Chapter 4, "Taxes and the Corporation as a Tax Shelter."

Perpetual Existence, Formality, and the Corporate Image
Unlike a sole proprietorship or partnership which ends with the death, disability, or withdrawal of the owner(s), a corporation may have a virtually unending life of its own. This aspect of the corporation is traditionally referred to as its "perpetual existence."

Of course, a corporation can be voluntarily terminated if the owner(s) choose(s) to dissolve it because of financial or personal reasons. Also, a bankruptcy proceeding, as mentioned previously, may result in involuntary dissolution. These exceptions notwithstanding, the corporation is a more stable form of business than the sole proprietorship or partnership because its life is independent of a particular owner or management team.

Besides increased stability, the corporate form also requires greater formality of business operation. This is the positive side to the larger number of regulations which govern corporations, as compared to other types of businesses. Symbolic of this increased formality is the use of the corporate seal on business agreements, such as the application for a corporate bank account or loan.[10]

The stability and formality of the corporate form will help to lend credence to your business in the eyes of creditors, banks, employees, and the like. Just as good will is an intangible yet very important asset to your business, so too does the corporate image play a valuable role.

If you are involved, for example, in consulting, free-lance writing, editing, advertising, or other types of loosely structured businesses, the Inc. after your company name may very well give you a decided edge over your competitors. The fact that you have chosen to incorporate will lend an aura of professionalism to you that often pays off literally in terms of increased sales and profits. The bottom line is that incorporating may be a wise investment in the area of intangible business assets, in addition to any other benefits realized.

Capitalizing the Corporation; Charitable Contributions

Two other areas unique to corporations are the special means at their disposal for raising money and their ability to deduct charitable contributions.

A closely held corporation can, of course, issue and sell additional shares of stock at any time in order to raise more capital. If your closely held corporation proves very successful in the market place, then at some point you may also consider "going public."

A public offering of stock can often provide hundreds of thousands or even millions of dollars in capital to growing corporations eager for expansion. If your stock is publicly traded, furthermore, you also have other avenues of financing open to you, through the issuance of corporate bonds (notes secured by company assets) and debentures (unsecured notes).

Corporations, unlike sole proprietors and partnerships, also have the right to deduct charitable contributions up to 10 percent of income each year (larger contributions can be carried over to future years and deducted from income). If you have a particular cause you want to support, then your corporation provides you an ideal tax-free means of doing so!

---

10   The seal is not legally required by Indiana law, but a place is designated for its impress on corporate business documents and on stock certificates. Although, technically speaking, its use is optional in the eyes of the state, you may be asked for it on formal business agreements, such as the application for a bank loan or even the application to open a corporate bank account. Seals can be ordered from many stationery stores. A corporate seal is also included with the Black Beauty Corporate Outfit available from The P. Gaines Co. (see the order form in the back of this book).

SUMMARY: MAJOR ADVANTAGES AND DISADVANTAGES OF INCORPORATING

Advantages

1. One of the greatest advantages of the corporate form is that the owner(s) of the corporation is (are) not personally liable for the debts of the corporation (taking into account the exceptions noted above—malpractice on the part of incorporated professionals; directorial fraud, malfeasance, or breach of fiduciary duty, loyalty, and care; unpaid taxes; and loans secured by personal assets).

2. The corporation as a tax shelter offers a number of tax-saving advantages not available to the sole proprietor or partnership, including lower tax brackets, [11] tax-free income in the form of medical reimbursements, pension and profit-sharing plans, "free" life, accident, and health insurance, tuition reimbursement plans paying up to $5,250 per employee for either work-related or non-work-related educational expenses, group legal services plans paying up to $70 per employee annually, and plans providing employees with dependent care assistance worth up to $5,000 per year tax-free.

3. The perpetual existence of the corporate entity gives it increased stability, enabling it to withstand changes in ownership or management.

4. Subject to certain limitations, a corporation may own shares in other corporations and receive dividends, 70 percent of which are tax free.

5. The stockholder(s)-owner(s) of a corporation can operate with all the benefits of a corporation but be taxed at personal income tax rates if this proves advantageous, as in the case of certain closely held family corporations (see Chapter 8, "The S Corporation").

6. The capital of the corporation can be increased with relative ease by issuing and selling to oneself or to other investors additional shares of stock. Corporations also have the option of making a public offering of stock and of raising capital through the issuance of corporate bonds and debentures.

7. As an employee, you can receive loans from your corporation.

8. The corporate image itself can be a valuable intangible business asset in your dealings with clients, employees, and banks.

9. Individuals receiving Social Security payments can use incorporation to escape the limits on earned income. In 1997, those 62 to 64 years of age can earn only $8,640 without penalty; the Social Security Administration will take $1 for each $2 earned above this limit. That amounts to a whopping 50 percent income tax rate on those earnings on top of the regular federal and state income taxes. For those between the ages of 65 and 69, each $3 of earned income above the limit of $13,500 reduces by $1 the individual's Social Security benefits (a 33 percent tax rate). By paying yourself no more than the limit in earned income and retaining the balance in the corporation, you would be able to withdraw the remaining income at age 70 when the limits on earned income no longer apply.

10. Under current law, one can use an S corporation to incorporate a stock portfolio or other passive income.

11. One surprising advantage of the corporate form for the small business person: chances of an IRS audit are substantially less if you incorporate! According to recent statistics, you are three times more likely to be audited by the IRS if you are a sole proprietor with more than $100,000 in annual in-

---

11   Although corporate income above $75,000 is taxed at the rate of 34 percent, the first $50,000 of that income is only taxed at 15 percent, and the next $25,000 at 25 percent.

come than if you are operating as a corporation with assets under $250,000.

Disadvantages

1. One small disadvantage of incorporation is the added expense you will pay in terms of fees, but these are extremely reasonable in Indiana: $90 for profit corporations, $30 for not for profit corporations. No franchise tax is collected by the state, except for financial institutions. In addition, profit corporations must file a biennial report and pay a filing fee of $30; not for profit corporations file an annual report with a $10 filing fee.

2. In order to use small claims courts in many states, corporations (unlike individuals, sole proprietors, and partnerships) must be represented by an attorney. This is a decided disadvantage for the incorporated small business person who uses or intends to use small claims court to collect unpaid bills and who wants to save money by doing his own collections. In Indiana, the law has been liberalized to allow a corporate officer to represent the corporation in court; attorneys are permitted to represent corporations, but are no longer required to do so. This "disadvantage" turns out to be an advantage instead, because of the legislative recognition of the unique needs of the small, incorporated business person in Indiana.

3. Unless your net taxable business earnings are at least $25,000, there may not be substantial tax advantages to incorporating (although other advantages, such as limitation of personal liability, will still hold). As a general rule, the higher your income, the more tax savings you will realize and the more fringe benefits you will be able to take advantage of as a corporation.

4. If you incorporate, you will pay more Social Security taxes than you would as a self-employed person (approximately 2 percent more, at present). On the plus side, these extra taxes are fully deductible by the corporation as a business expense, but not by the self-employed individual. (Since 1990, however, when the self-employment rate and the combined employer-employee corporate rate of Social Security tax each equalled 15.3 percent, self-employers have been able to deduct half their self-employment tax as a business expense.)

The current higher rate of Social Security tax paid by corporations will not result in any extra Social Security benefits when you retire. In the case of a wife working for the incorporated business, the couple's combined Social Security taxes may seem doubly burdensome. Since a low-income spouse will receive more, upon retirement, from the spousal benefits derived from her husband's account than she will from her own account, her Social Security benefits are, in a sense, wasted, although required by law.

In other circumstances, she will stand to benefit, however. In the event of her death, her minor children can collect benefits on her account. She may also choose to retire and start collecting Social Security benefits while her husband continues working. If the marriage does not last at least 10 years, furthermore, she cannot draw on benefits from her husband's account, so she will need her own retirement plan. Since, according to one study, the average marriage today lasts only about 9 years, the additional Social Security tax paid by the corporation on behalf of a working spouse may turn out to be a blessing in disguise.

5. You will be required to pay an unemployment tax to the state and federal governments to cover yourself as an employee of the corporation.

6. The increased paperwork in maintaining the corporate records and in filing two tax returns (individual and corporate) will be another price of doing business as a corporation. Since 1984, most small corporations have been able to file the short-form federal corporation return (Form 1120-A), so this simplifies matters somewhat. The state of Indiana also requires the filing of an annual corporate income tax return. If you are knowledgeable about tax laws and normally file your own tax returns, you may well be able to continue doing so for your corporation. If not, you will need to hire a tax preparer or accountant to handle the filings.

7. If you are already operating a business as a sole proprietor or as a member of a partnership, you may incur certain relatively minor expenses in notifying the public of your new status as a corporation, such as changing your telephone listings, having new stationery printed, and so on.

8. The fee charged by an attorney for an incorporation averages out to be around $1,000. Those willing to invest the time and energy to set up their own corporation, even if they have their incorporation papers reviewed by a lawyer, can still save most of these costs. Approximately one-third of all new corporations are formed without a lawyer, so if you decide to go it on your own, you are not alone!

TO INCORPORATE OR NOT . . .

We have given an overview of the corporation as a form of business ownership, in contrast to the sole proprietorship, the partnership, and the limited liability company, and have discussed some of the major advantages and disadvantages of incorporating. Subsequent chapters will deal in greater detail with the various topics introduced here. Before reaching a decision in your individual case on whether or not to incorporate, be sure to consider all the pros and cons. Plan to consult an attorney, particularly if there are special aspects to your situation.

CHAPTER 2. INDIANA CORPORATIONS

The first chapter was intended to acquaint you with the operation of corporations in general. In this chapter, we will focus on the Indiana corporation.

Purposes of a Corporation

The Indiana Business Corporation Law (BCL) which went into effect on July 1, 1987, streamlined the process of setting up a corporation in this state. This Act, with annual updates and revisions, has become a model for other states that want to encourage the formation and operation of new businesses. The Indiana corporation law provides greater ease of establishing a corporation and greater flexibility in running one. The BCL defines the types of profit corporations that may be set up in the state and the laws governing their conduct. It is this Act that the following discussion will highlight.

This particular Act does not apply to foreign banking, surety, trust, safe deposit, railroad, insurance, and building and loan corporations; these types of businesses do not need to obtain a certificate of authority from the Secretary of State under the Business Corporation Law to transact business in Indiana because they are governed by special corporation statutes.

Two kinds of corporations with unique characteristics and their own special provisions for organization in Indiana will be treated in this book in later chapters. These include the Professional Service Corporation (discussed in Chapter 6) and the Not for Profit Corporation (discussed in Chapter 7).

In Section 23-1-22-1 of the Indiana Business Corporation Law, the broad range of purposes for Indiana corporations is defined as follows:

Every corporation incorporated under this article has the purpose of engaging in any lawful business unless a more limited purpose is set forth in the articles of incorporation.

Any "lawful" activity, then, may be incorporated in Indiana under the Business Corporation Law, with the exceptions noted. In filling out the Articles of Incorporation (see Appendix A in the back of this book), you do not need to describe or even specify the type of business you are incorporating.[1] It

---

1 In the past, Not for Profit Corporations and Professional Corporations required specific purpose clauses in the Articles of Incorporation, but even these types of corporations no longer have to spell out their purposes in the Articles.

is automatically assumed, unless a different purpose is stated in the Articles of Incorporation, that the purpose of the corporation will simply be "the transaction of any or all lawful business activities for which corporations may be organized under the Indiana Business Corporation Law."

We will focus on the general for-profit corporation in the remainder of this chapter.

Powers of Profit Corporations

Section 23-1-22-2 of the Indiana Business Corporation Law spells out the particular activities Indiana corporations are authorized to engage in. In spite of the legalese of the language, we suggest you read this list carefully. This will give you an appreciation of the types of power your corporation will enjoy in the event you incorporate your business.

1. To have perpetual duration, unless a limited period of duration is stated in the corporation's Articles of Incorporation.

2. To sue and be sued, complain and defend in its corporate name, in like manner as an individual person.

3. To have and alter at will a corporate seal and use it by causing it or a facsimile to be affixed, impressed, or reproduced in any other manner. However, the use of a corporate seal or an impression is not required and does not affect the validity of any instrument whatsoever, notwithstanding any other statutes.

4. To make and amend bylaws, including emergency bylaws (see section 23-1-21-7), not inconsistent with its Articles of Incorporation or with the laws of this state, for managing the business and regulating the affairs of the corporation.

5. To purchase, receive, lease, or otherwise acquire and own, hold, improve, use, and otherwise deal with real or personal property, or any legal or equitable interest in property, wherever located.

6. To sell, convey, exchange, mortgage, pledge, lease and otherwise dispose of all or any part of its property.

7. To be a promoter, partner, member, associate, or manager of any partnership, joint venture, trust, or other entity.

8. To purchase, receive, subscribe for, or otherwise acquire, own, hold, vote, use, sell, mortgage, lend, pledge, or otherwise dispose of and deal in and with shares or other interests in, or obligations of, any entity, including itself, except as otherwise prohibited by this article.

9. To make contracts, give guarantees, and incur liabilities; to borrow money, issue its notes, bonds, and other obligations (which may be convertible into or include the option to purchase other securities of the corporation), and secure any of its obligations by mortgage or pledge of any of its property, franchises, or income.

10. To lend money, invest and reinvest its funds, and receive and hold real and personal property as security for repayment.

11. To make donations for the public welfare or for charitable, educational, or scientific purposes.

12. To conduct its business, locate offices, and exercise the powers granted by this article within or without Indiana.

13. To elect directors, elect and appoint officers, and appoint employees and other agents of the corporation, define their duties, fix their compensation and lend them money and credit.

14. To pay pensions and establish and administer pension plans, profit sharing plans, sharing plans, share bonus plans, share option plans, welfare plans,

24

qualified and nonqualified retirement plans, and benefit or incentive plans for any or all of its current or former directors, officers, employees, and agents.

15. To transact any lawful business that will aid governmental policy; and

16. To make payments or donations, or do any other act, not inconsistent with law, that furthers the business and affairs of the corporation.

The Eyes and the Ears of the Corporation

Since the corporation is a fictitious person, the actual work of the corporation must be carried on by real people. These individuals who conduct the business of the corporation fall into four basic categories,[2] according to their roles:

Incorporators
Directors
Officers
Shareholders

Many corporations will also have other employees or workers, in addition to the officers who run the business on a day-to-day basis. In a one-man or one-woman corporation, a single individual will play all these parts. Wanda Gold may wear all the hats at Wanda Gold Enterprises, Inc. In a larger corporation, these jobs will be divided among separate individuals. Even here there is generally some overlapping, however, particularly between the board of directors and officers of the corporation. At A.T.&T., for example, Robert Allen served for years as both chairman of the board of directors and chief executive officer (president).

Incorporators

The incorporators, also referred to in common parlance as the "promoters"[3] of the corporation, are the persons who sign the Articles of Incorporation and who make practical arrangements to set up the corporation. Such arrangements may include a broad canopy of activities, from drawing up employment contracts and leasing office space to naming the initial board of directors. (It is advisable, for legal reasons, however, to postpone making employment contracts, renting office space, and entering into other types of contractual agreements until after the corporation has been formed.) Although we have referred to "incorporators," the minimum number of such individuals required by Indiana law is at present only one. Unlike some states, there is no minimum age limit for incorporators in Indiana.

The incorporator(s) is (are) responsible for raising start-up capital for the corporation. Some states specify a minimum amount of capital which a corporation must raise before commencing business. Indiana, following the trend of other states, such as New York, California, and Illinois,

---

2   These categories exist in virtually *all* corporations, but we are concerned in the following discussion primarily with the specific delimitations of these categories in the Indiana statutes.

3   While most small corporations are formed by individuals, it is important to note that, under Indiana law, a partnership or a corporation (whether domestic or foreign, profit or not for profit) may also act as incorporator of an Indiana corporation.

no longer specifies by law a minimum dollar amount as a prerequisite to incorporating.

From a practical standpoint, however, most any business will require working capital. From a legal standpoint, your corporation should have at least enough capital to begin operations and to pay foreseeable, short-range expenses. If not, your "thin" (undercapitalized) corporation may run into legal problems, resulting in your being subjected to personal liability by the courts for the corporation's unpaid debts. If you already have an existing business, then as incorporator you can transfer assets from it in return for shares of stock.[4]

In the event that you are starting your Indiana corporation from scratch, you will need either to provide seed money from your personal funds (a portion of which may be in the form of loans to the corporation) or to find investors to capitalize the corporation in exchange for stock. Later in this chapter we will look at the role of the stockholder, whether that of the incorporator herself or other investors.

If initial directors are not named in the Articles of Incorporation, then it falls to the incorporator or incorporators to hold an organizational meeting, at the call of a majority of incorporators, to elect a board of directors, who shall complete the organization of the corporation. If, however, a corporation under Indiana Code section 23-1-33-1(c) will not have a board of directors, the subscribers (shareholders) shall hold an organizational meeting to complete the organization of the corporation.

Directors
The board of directors (which may consist of a single director in Indiana) oversees the business operations of the corporation. The number of directors shall be fixed by, or in the manner provided in, the bylaws, unless the Articles of Incorporation fix the number. Section 23-1-33-1 provides that corporations having 50 or fewer shareholders may dispense with the board of directors entirely or limit the authority of the board by describing in its Articles of Incorporation who will perform some or all the duties of the board of directors. In the case of such small corporations (usually referred to as "close corporations" or "closely held corporations") that do not have a board of directors, one or more shareholders typically manage the corporation under a so-called "shareholders' agreement."

If initial directors are named in the Articles of Incorporation, the initial directors shall hold an organizational meeting, at the call of the majority of directors, to complete the organization of the corporation, by electing or appointing officers, adopting bylaws, and carrying on any other business brought before the meeting (See "First Meeting of Board of Directors," pages 65-68).

The duties of the board of directors ordinarily include making major policy decisions and managing the distribution of money. The board of directors typically

---

4   See Chapter 5 for specific recommendations regarding the transfer of assets from an existing business and start-up loans for your corporation.

decides when and how much the company will pay out in dividends to its stockholders and how much will remain in the company for its capital needs, research and development, ordinary business expenses, and so on.

Directors of Indiana corporations do not have to be of a set age or residents of this state. While there are no mandatory requirements for directors under the Business Corporation Law, desired qualifications for directors may be stated in the Articles of Incorporation or the corporate bylaws. It is common practice for directors to serve without pay, since their work is ordinarily performed in order to increase the value of their stock holdings in the corporation. Directors in Indiana do not have to be stockholders, however, so financial compensation (including pension, disability, and death benefits) is permitted by law as long as it is given for real services. In addition, directorial salaries should be authorized in advance at a meeting of the board of directors, subject to approval of the shareholders only if the Articles of Incorporation so provide.

Traditionally, the board of directors meets once a month, although the small corporation opting to have a board of directors can often get by with one annual meeting (usually held on the same day as, and immediately after, the annual shareholders' meeting). Of course, special meetings may also be called at any time during the year in order to document a formal resolution, for instance, a directors' resolution authorizing a bank loan. Informal meetings or even phone conferences may also be held to decide a particular issue. In such cases, all the directors must sign a written consent setting forth the action so taken and include these consents with the minutes of the directors' meetings or file them with the corporate records.

Special meetings shall be held upon notice as prescribed in the Articles of Incorporation or bylaws. A majority of directors is necessary to constitute a quorum for a meeting of directors, and the act of a majority of the directors present at the meeting is the act of the board unless the act of a greater number is required by the Articles of Incorporation, or the corporate bylaws. The Indiana Business Corporation Law (section 23-1-34-5) specifies that the Articles of Incorporation or bylaws may also authorize a quorum of a board of directors to consist of no *fewer* than 1/3 of the fixed or prescribed number of directors. Unless the Articles of Incorporation provide otherwise, only a corporation's board of directors may amend or repeal the corporation's bylaws.

Appendix D contains forms for the Minutes of the First Meeting of the board of directors. Recommended instructions for filling out these forms are included in Chapter 5. Even if you are the only director/officer of the corporation, you are required to keep minutes for the first and all subsequent director meetings and file them permanently with the corporate records (unless you choose to dispense with the board of directors and state in the Articles of Incorporation who will perform their roles). They contain vital information about your company regarding annual compensation, the issuance of stock, new or amended corporate bylaws, the election of officers, and so on.

The directors are always elected by the stockholders. This election may be a mere formality when the corporation has only one or two stockholders who choose themselves as directors. In a large corporation, this is one of the main functions of the stockholders, to vote for the board of directors.

The Indiana Business Corporation Law provides for one-year terms for directors, with annual elections each year unless their terms are to be staggered under section 23-1-33-6, which provides for two- or three-year terms under different circumstances. If the Articles of Incorporation or bylaws do not specify the terms of directors, however, each director shall hold office until the next annual meeting of shareholders and until her successor is elected, or until her earlier resignation, removal from office, or death. Since the Indiana statutes do not forbid a director from running for re-election, you may continue to elect the same director(s) year after year. Further discussion of the voting procedures for the election of directors will follow in the section on "Shareholders" hereafter.

Directors may resign by submitting written notice to the board of directors, its chairman, or the secretary of the corporation. In closely held corporations, vacancies on the board of directors are normally filled by shareholder vote, whereas in publicly held corporations vacancies are often filled by the board itself.

Directors may be removed in any manner provided in the Articles of Incorporation. Unless otherwise provided by the Articles of Incorporation, a director or the entire board may be removed, with or without cause, by vote of the holders of a majority of the shares entitled to vote at an election of directors. A director may be removed by the shareholders, if they are otherwise authorized to do so, only at a meeting called for the purpose of removing the director and the meeting notice must state that the purpose, or one of the purposes, of the meeting is removal of the director (section 23-1-33-8 [d]).

Directors may also propose dissolution of the corporation in the event of: bankruptcy; the expiration of the period of existence of a limited-life corporation specified in its Articles of Incorporation; the cancellation of the Articles for failure to file biennial reports or pay taxes due; for failure to notify the Secretary of State within 60 days that the corporation's registered agent has resigned or its registered office has been discontinued or either has changed. In Indiana, the directors alone may initiate dissolution, but the proposal must be presented to the shareholders for a vote.

Officers

The primary officers of a corporation ordinarily consist of a president, a secretary, and a treasurer, and, if desired, one or more vice-presidents. Other officers or assistants may also be elected or appointed, as needed, as specified in the bylaws. Unless otherwise provided in the Articles of Incorporation or bylaws, the officers shall be elected or appointed by the board of directors.

None of the officers need be a director, but, in a small, closely held corporation, some, if not all, of the officers will undoubtedly be chosen from among the directors.

28

The officers are in charge of running the corporation on a day-to-day basis. Therefore, a large corporation will require many more officers than a small corporation. The exact duties of the officers are either defined in the corporate bylaws or by the board of directors or by direction of an officer authorized by the board of directors to prescribe the duties of other officers. To avoid confusion, the bylaws should state the officer titles of your corporation as well as their duties, which, of course, may be customized according to the particular needs of your business. Generic descriptions of the usual four—president, vice-president, secretary, and treasurer—are included in the sample bylaws in Appendix B.

In Indiana, the law requires that a corporation must have at least one officer. If the bylaws or Articles of Incorporation so provide, any two or more offices may be held by the same person. An officer elected or appointed shall hold office for the term for which he is elected or appointed and until his successor is elected or appointed and qualified, or until his resignation or removal.

Officers are elected or appointed in a manner and at a time provided in the bylaws. The sample bylaws in Appendix B specify officer elections by the board of directors, at either an annual meeting or a special meeting. An officer elected or appointed by the board may be removed with or without cause. An officer who appoints another officer or assistant officer may remove the appointed officer or assistant officer at any time with or without cause. An officer may also resign by delivering written notice to the corporation's board of directors, its

chairman, or the secretary of the corporation.

Our friend Wanda as sole director-shareholder, for example, may hold all four offices of president, vice-president, secretary, and treasurer of Wanda Gold Enterprises, Inc., if the bylaws or Articles so allow. If her brother Junior is also willing to serve as an officer, they may decide to divide these four positions between them. Wanda, for instance, can be (1) president and vice-president (in theory, although in reality this combination would not be a good choice, since the vice-president normally substitutes for the president in his or her absence) or (2) president and treasurer or (3) vice-president and secretary or (4) secretary and treasurer or (5) vice-president and treasurer, or (6) president and secretary of the corporation, with Junior holding the other two offices remaining in each case. Or Wanda may choose to hold three offices and Junior one, or vice versa. If their mother Giesela is also an officer, then the three of them can divide up the four positions any way they choose. There is a wide range of flexibility in this area.

As in the case of directors, a sole stockholder-director does not have to hold all the offices unless he chooses to do so. He can find other persons to fill additional offices if he so desires, by enlisting other relatives, friends, business acquaintances as officers. Or you may wish to designate that your corporation will have only one executive office, which you yourself will fill.

As noted above, sample bylaws which define the duties of the main traditional offices of president, vice-president, secretary, and treasurer are included in Appendix B, with the provision that the board may create other offices considered necessary. The president is the chief executive officer who directs the business affairs of the corporation. He or she has the power to bind the corporation in contracts and in debt obligations. Other duties, such as the power to hire and fire employees, vary from one corporation to another and should be spelled out in the bylaws.

The vice-president assumes the duties of the president in case of his or her absence or disability and performs other duties as prescribed by the board of directors. Unlike the president, however, he or she does not normally have the power to bind the corporation unless authorized to do so in a specific circumstance.

The secretary keeps the minutes of all the meetings of the directors and shareholders and is in charge of the bylaws of the corporation and the share register showing the names and addresses of the shareholders. The secretary also notifies the shareholders and directors of meetings, has charge of the corporate seal, and assumes other duties specified by the president or the board of directors.

The treasurer keeps the account books of the corporation, makes deposits of money, pays creditors, and prepares and presents financial reports on the corporation to the president and board of directors. The manner and nature of performance of the duties of the corporate officers are subject to the final authority of the directors.

The salaries of the officers are set by the board of directors, subject to approval of the shareholders if the Articles of Incor-poration or bylaws so provide. As in the case of the salaries of directors, compensation must be reasonable and given for real services to the corporation. If your business chooses not to pay its stockholder-officers a salary but opts instead to repay their efforts on behalf of the corporation exclusively through stock dividends, the bylaws should so state.

Shareholders

Like the limited partners of a partnership agreement, the shareholders of a corporation are under no obligation to the creditors of the corporation or to the corporation itself, beyond paying the full amount due for shares they purchase. If Wanda Gold is the sole shareholder of her company, as shareholder she has no legal obligation to the corporation after paying for her stock. It is in her additional role as director and officer that she owes the corporation a fiduciary duty. That is, she must look out for the best interests of the corporation, act honestly in her business dealings with it, give the corporation the right of first refusal, etc.

Besides providing capital and thus, quite literally, owning the corporation, the shareholders have several other functions as well. Most importantly, as already pointed out, they vote for the board of directors. Each outstanding share of the corporation is entitled to one vote, unless otherwise provided in the Articles of Incorporation, and, except as otherwise provided in the Articles, directors shall be elected by a plurality of the votes cast by the shares entitled to vote in the election at a meeting at which a quorum is present.

Under Indiana Code section 23-1-33-1(c), a corporation may choose not to have a board of directors. In such a case, the shareholders shall hold an organizational meeting to complete the organization of the corporation, according to the plan in Chapter 5 (See "First Meeting of Board of Directors," pages 65-68).

In Indiana, the Articles of Incorporation may provide for cumulative voting. Under cumulative voting procedures, each shareholder has the right to cumulate such voting power as he possesses and to give one directorial candidate as many votes as the number of directors to be elected multiplied by the number of his shares equals, or to divide his votes on the same principle between two or more candidates as he so desires.

The purpose of cumulative voting is to protect the interest of minority stockholders. An example will show how it works. Take the case of Joe Stockholder, who owns 20 shares of stock in Wonder Widgets, Inc., a closely held Indiana corporation which presently has three positions on the board of directors to be filled. If cumulative voting procedures are in effect, Joe will have 60 votes to cast in whatever manner he wishes. If Mary Public, the only other stockholder in the same corporation, owns 30 shares, her total voting power will amount to 90 votes.

Even though Joe is a minority shareholder, by cumulating all of his 60 votes for one candidate, Joe has the ability to elect at least one representative to the board of directors, while Mary has sufficient votes to elect the other two. Without cumulative voting, however, Joe would receive *no* representation on the board of directors, since Mary would always be able to outvote him under normal voting procedures. Joe does not, by the way, have to pool all of his votes behind one candidate. He can use his votes in any combination that he desires, dividing them among two or even three candidates. Only by voting all of his shares for one candidate, however, can he be assured of electing his own man (or woman!) to the board.

Cumulative voting, if it is, in fact, provided for in the Articles of Incorporation, can only be used for the election of directors to the board. Cumulative voting *cannot* be employed for other matters brought before the shareholders for a vote.

Regarding cumulative voting procedures, the Indiana statutes specify that a shareholder who has the right to cumulate his or her votes must give notice to the corporation not less than 48 hours before the time set for the meeting of the shareholder's intent to cumulate the shareholder's votes during the meeting, and if one shareholder gives this notice, all other shareholders in the same voting group participating in the election are entitled to cumulate their votes without giving further notice (Section 23-1-30-9 [d][1]).

Two types of shareholder meeting are authorized by the Indiana Business Corporation Law: an annual meeting, at a time and place fixed in the corporation's bylaws, and special meetings, called by the board of directors or by the holders of at least 25 percent of the votes (in corporations with 50 or fewer shareholders). Shareholders may take corporate action without a meeting as well, by means of written consents.

Shareholders also have certain other rights defined by the BCL. Shareholders' approval by a majority is required for mergers and consolidations of the corporation with another in certain situations and for the amendment of the Articles of Incorporation under certain circumstances (see sections 23-1-38-3 and 4). In addition, voluntary dissolution of the corporation must be approved by a majority vote of the shareholders, provided the board of directors has proposed that dissolution be considered. Just as the shareholders participate in the profits of the corporation through dividends, so too would they share in the distribution of the assets of the corporation upon voluntary or involuntary dissolution.

Sale of Stock

The Indiana Business Corporation Law specifies that corporate stock may be paid in any tangible or intangible property or benefit to the corporation, including cash, promissory notes,[5] services performed, contracts for services to be performed, or other securities of the corporation.

This initial amount of payment for stock can be in cash or in other assets, including equipment (for example, a truck, restaurant fixtures, tables and chairs), inventories, accounts receivable, etc. Therefore, if you as sole owner of a business have capital assets consisting of any combination of cash and/or property, then you can exchange all, or a portion of, these assets for stock to begin business as a corporation. During the course of your operation as a corporation, you may take part of your compensation for actual work performed in the form of additional shares of stock. This is a common practice of many business executives of both small and large corporations, enabling them frequently to amass large stock portfolios.

On the Indiana Articles of Incorporation form, you are not asked to specify the type of stock to be issued, whether common or preferred and the par value, if any (unless you choose to have more than one class of stock). A little background information may nevertheless prove helpful.

The par value of a preferred stock represents the dollar value on which the stock's dividend is based. For instance, a 10 percent preferred, $20 par value stock would pay an annual dividend of $2.00 per share (10 percent of $20). Most small corporations do not issue preferred stock. however.

In regard to common stock, par value is an arbitrary amount which may be assigned to each share of a company's common stock under the company's charter issued by the state when it incorporates. It is primarily a

5   If a corporation authorizes the issuance of shares for promissory notes or for promises to render services in the future, the corporation shall report in writing to the shareholders the number of shares authorized to be so issued with or before the notice of the next shareholders' meeting (section 23-1-53-2).

bookkeeping device. Stock with a par value of, say, $10 cannot be sold for less than its face value, whereas no-par value stock can be sold at any value set by the board of directors or shareholders.

It is ordinarily simpler for most small corporations to issue common, no par-value stock, due to the greater leeway in allocating funds within the corporation from the sale of this type of stock.[6]

The Indiana Articles of Incorporation form does ask the incorporator to specify the number of shares of stock authorized. Theoretically, this number can be almost anything, for instance, from 1 to 100,000 shares of common stock might be authorized. In practice, however, we recommend the following guideline: **The number of authorized shares should be greater than the number actually issued.**

If you authorized 1,000 common shares but issued only 100 shares of the authorized number for a consideration of $10,000 of stated capital, you would later be able to make additional issues of shares without further report to the Secretary of State.[7] In this way, you can increase the capital of your corporation in the future if need be by issuing and buying additional shares of stock yourself. Or you may decide to sell shares to other investors, reward an employee with a gift of stock, or transfer part of the ownership of the company to other family members through donations of stock.

The Indiana Business Corporation Law permits corporations to have different classes of stock, such as voting and non-voting. These rights and limitations must be spelled out in the Articles of Incorporation; otherwise, every share of stock is entitled to vote. In the past, you were not allowed under federal law to adopt Subchapter S status, discussed in Chapter 8, if your corporation had both voting and non-voting stock. The Subchapter S Revision Act of 1982 has eliminated this requirement, however, effective January 1, 1983. Some family corporations who want to keep control of the corporation within the hands of several family members while giving other family members (say, their children or retired parents) shares of stock may want to devise voting and non-voting classes of stock. Legal counsel is advisable in such a case.

---

6 In the case of par-value stock, if the face value is $10 and the stock sells for $12, $10 of every $12 received as payment must go into the capital reserves; the $2 excess constitutes capital surplus. In the case of no par-value stock, gains from its sale may be allocated between stated capital and capital surplus in any proportion decided by the board.

7 No further report (and filing expense) would be required as long as you did not issue more shares than the number authorized in the original Articles of Incorporation. It pays to plan ahead. If you do later wish to authorize additional shares, a certificate of amendment to the Articles must be approved by the shareholders of the corporation and filed with the Secretary of State, along with a filing fee.

Chapter 3. SHOULD I FORM A DELAWARE CORPORATION?

There are a number of books on the market today which advocate forming a Delaware corporation, regardless of which state you live and do business in. These books are invariably written and published by Delaware companies who want to sell you their services as "registered agents."[1]

Nevada, like Delaware, is another state that actively courts out-of-state businesses to incorporate in Nevada. There is nothing illegal about forming a Delaware or Nevada corporation, even if you are doing business exclusively in Indiana. Whether it is advisable is another question. An objective look at the issue of whether a Delaware corporation is recommended for the Indiana small business person follows.

In the past, certain businesses in Indiana and other states did find it advantageous to incorporate out of state because of tax and legal loopholes. All states, including Indiana, have now closed these loopholes. You cannot avoid Indiana taxes and fees by forming a Delaware corporation, as we shall see.

Those publications which recommend Delaware corporations sometimes imply that persons residing in other states with minimum capitalization requirements can bypass these requirements by means of a Delaware corporation, since Delaware has no minimum capital requirement for beginning a corporation. Indiana, like Delaware, does not fix by law a specific minimum capitalization for new corporations. You don't have to ante up a specific amount of money to launch your new corporation, in other words. Delaware corporations, therefore, do not hold an advantage over Indiana ones in this regard.

In reality, no one ordinarily starts a corporation without any capital whatsoever. This is a very risky proposition, from both a financial and a legal standpoint. (See the discussion of "thin" corporations in the previous chapter.) Even in states that do have minimum capital requirements (generally a $500 or $1,000 minimum), this minimum is certainly a bare minimum. Almost all businesses would require more than this sum as start-up working capital.

---

1   If you form a Delaware corporation but your business is located in another state, you would require a registered agent with a Delaware mailing address who would forward your Delaware Articles of Incorporation, annual reports, and other official papers from the state of Delaware to you.

One conceivable case in which you might choose to form an out-of-state corporation is if you are under 18 years of age and reside in a state that requires incorporators to be at least 18 years old. Currently, some 30 states do have such an age requirement, while several others specify only that the incorporator must be "capable to contract." Indiana is not one of these states that does have a minimum age requirement for incorporators, however. Delaware corporation law thus provides no advantage over Indiana law in this respect either.[2]

In summary, we began by observing that in the past it was advantageous for some Indiana businesses to incorporate out of state. Most frequently, these out-of-state corporations were formed in Delaware, because of the simplicity of the corporate laws and low fees in that state. Due to changes in the laws governing foreign corporations, there are very few cases where a Delaware corporation would now benefit an Indiana business person.

The only exceptions to this general rule are very large, publicly traded corporations, which operate interstate or internationally. These types of corporations may gain certain technical advantages in such areas as voting rights by incorporating in Delaware. Some companies initially incorporate or later re-incorporate in Delaware because Delaware corporate regulations sometimes make it easier for a company to defend against unwanted takeovers, for example. This is obviously not a problem that small, privately held Indiana corporations have to worry about. For the Indiana business person with capitalization under $500,000, a Delaware corporation is *not* recommended.

The distinct *disadvantage* of a Delaware corporation is, of course, that it will cost you additional, unnecessary time and expense, if you are doing business in Indiana (not Delaware). If you form a Delaware corporation, you will have to register in Indiana as a foreign corporation, as already mentioned. As a foreign corporation, you will have to obtain a certificate of authority to do business in Indiana and pay the same fee as an Indiana domestic corporation ($90) and the same amount of annual tax on income and assets.

Don't forget, however, that in addition you will have to pay Delaware license or filing fees and franchise taxes as well. These are not just extra, one-time expenses. You will be paying these Delaware franchise taxes as well as annual report fees yearly. Unless you plan to open an office in Delaware, you will also have to hire a registered agent to provide you with a Delaware mailing address. In general, those who advocate Delaware corporations for anyone and everyone are putting a large number of individuals to additional ex-

---

2   Even if you reside in a state that requires you to be 18 years of age or older to legally act as an incorporator, such a requirement comprises no real obstacle to setting up your own corporation if you are a minor. Incorporators do not have to be stockholders. Consequently, you can have an adult file the incorporation papers for you (a lawyer, parent or friend, for example). This is a perfectly acceptable procedure which would allow you to be sole stockholder of a corporation if you so choose even if you are legally a minor.

pense and paperwork, with no offsetting advantages.

Also, if you form a Delaware corporation and fail to obtain a certificate of authority to do business in Indiana as a foreign corporation from the Indiana Secretary of State, you will be denied the use of the court system of this state for the purpose of initiating civil actions and may be personally liable for business debts and lawsuits. If you later decide to pay the fee, you will then be allowed to use the courts. It is important to note that a foreign corporation conducting affairs in the state without a certificate of authority is also liable for a penalty of up to $10,000.00 (Indiana Code § 23-1-49-2[d]). All amounts due shall be recovered with costs in an action prosecuted by the Attorney General.

In short, unless you are actually planning to conduct your business in another state, it is easier, cheaper, and smarter for you to incorporate in Indiana.

Chapter 4. TAXES AND THE CORPORATION AS A TAX SHELTER

The tax man cometh, not only for you and me personally but also for corporations. In this chapter, we will consider the various taxes paid by Indiana corporations as well as some of the main ways of minimizing taxes through the corporate form of business ownership. Clearly, the corporation is the most advantageous type of business when it comes to minimizing taxes. When you incorporate, your salary is tax-deductible, your medical coverage (including insurance premiums) is deductible, your disability insurance premium is deductible, most of your life insurance premium is deductible, and practically all other business-related expenses are deductible.

Indiana State Taxes

Corporate Franchise Tax and Biennial Report

Indiana had no corporate franchise tax until 1990, when a 4 percent franchise tax, applicable only to financial institutions such as banks, was instituted.

Under Indiana law, corporations must file a biennial report (due every other year) with the Secretary of State and pay a filing fee of $30. Corporations formed in an even year file every even year; corporations formed in an odd year file every odd year.

This report, which asks you to verify and update information about the corporate registered office and registered agent, the corporate officers and directors' names and addresses, the total number of authorized shares of the corporation, and similar matters, is due in the month in which the corporation was originally organized. If you incorporated your business in May 1997, for instance, your biennial reports would be due by May 31 in the years 1999, 2001, 2003, 2005, etc. [1]

Failure to file the biennial report and pay the filing fee will result in dissolution of your corporation by the Secretary of State.

State Corporate Tax

The Indiana corporate income tax rate can run from a low of .3 percent of Indiana gross receipts to a high of 3.4 percent of adjusted gross income, depending on a number of factors. A suplemental net income tax of 4.5 percent of a portion of a corporation's adjusted gross income is also added on.

---

1   Each corporation should automatically receive its biennial report form and notification of fee owed at least 30 days prior to the month in which the report is due.

The income of the corporation is subject to certain credits that would reduce its tax, such as the neighborhood assistance credit for investments in qualified neighborhood assistance programs; credit for use of qualified energy systems; credit for employing inmates within correctional facilities; credit for lending money to entities in "enterprise zones" and/or investing in enterprise zones, industrial recovery sites, and drug and alcohol abuse prevention programs; credit for donating computer hardware or software to schools; credit for hiring math and science teachers during summer recess; credit for donations to accredited Indiana colleges and universities; credit for owning and operating a maternity home in Indiana.[2]

The Indiana corporate income tax return is Form IT-20, due by the fifteenth day of the fourth month following the close of the tax year (April 15 for calendar year corporations). S corporations in the state file an information return, IT-20S. While most S corporations are exempt from Indiana corporate income tax, an S corporation that is liable for the federal capital gains tax under Section 1374 and/or net passive investment income tax under Section 1375 of the Internal Revenue Code, will be liable for Indiana corporate income tax. (Regarding how the income of S corporations is treated for tax purposes, see Chapter 8, "The Subchapter S Corporation").

State Sales Tax

Both incorporated and unincorporated Indiana businesses are required to pay sales taxes to the state, collected on retail sales. It is actually the consumer, not the business, who pays these taxes, but you as a business owner-operator are responsible for collecting the taxes in an orderly fashion and remitting them to the state at regular intervals.

The Indiana sales tax rate is currently 5 percent on retail sales over 90¢; qualifying food, drugs, medical appliances, and certain other items are exempt from tax (see Indiana Code §6-2.5-5-1 to 33 for a complete list of items exempted from sales tax).

Individual State Income Tax

Any profits distributed to individual shareholders during the year as dividends must be reported on the state personal income tax returns (Form IT-40) of the recipients. These dividends are taxed at the rate of all income in Indiana, presently a rate of 3.4 percent. This tax rate is subject to certain tax credits, including credits for donations to higher education and 21st Century Scholars Program, for being 65 years of age or older and having a federal adjusted income of less than $10,000 for the taxable year.

---

2   Another category exists under Indiana law, that of corporations that operate as regular corporations but could qualify under federal law to be S corporations and whose passive investment income is less than 25 percent of gross income. See Chapter 8 of this book for a complete list of qualifications for an S corporation. Indiana corporations meeting these qualifications file Form IT-20SC and are exempt from one type of Indiana income tax (the so-called gross income tax). Most small Indiana corporations will fall into this category and can file Form IT-20SC and pay less tax.

Since dividends are taxed at both the corporate and individual level, this results in the famous so-called "double taxation" of corporations. You will want to take this fact into consideration when deciding if and when and how much in dividends to pay the stockholder(s) of the corporation. For most small corporations, double taxation is not a worry, since dividends do not have to be paid at all, unless the corporation accumulates in excess of $250,000 in assets. Most small corporations will pay out almost all their earnings in salaries and fringe benefits, and will pay *no* dividends at all. Such a typical situation does not result in any double taxation.

It is usually preferable to take money out of your corporation in ways other than paying dividends, as long as you are not violating the law. More will be said about this issue later in this chapter. Under certain circumstances, you will be *required* by law to issue dividends. The IRS has set a ceiling on the amount of money that can accumulate in the company at lower corporate tax rates without being distributed as dividends.

For professional service corporations, such as the health professions and engineering, the limit of accumulated earnings is currently $150,000. For other types of corporations, the limit is set at $250,000. Certain exceptions, such as the need for additional capital to expand your business or purchase another, are allowed.

A hefty tax penalty is imposed on businesses that exceed their capital accumulations limit without any justification. The corporate minutes of meetings will normally lay the groundwork of plans for expansion, contingency funding, and similar rationales for accumulating capital in excess of the normal limits set by the IRS. The problem with many corporations will be simply in reaching these limits, not in exceeding them!

The legal power to declare dividends rests solely with the board of directors, subject to Indiana laws. In some cases defined by the Indiana statutes, a corporation is not permitted to pay dividends.

Basically, dividends cannot be declared or paid at a time when the corporation is insolvent or when the payment of dividends would make the corporation insolvent or reduce its net assets to less than zero or when the payment would be contrary to any restriction contained in the Articles of Incorporation. See §23-1-28-3 for the statute limitations on issuing corporate dividends in Indiana.

Directors who authorized dividends when dividends are not permitted under §23-1-28-3 are held personally liable for their actions. If your corporation will have to pay large dividends to its shareholders on a regular basis, you may consider electing Subchapter S corporate status (See Chapter 8, "The S Corporation").

Federal Taxes

Corporate Income Tax

As pointed out previously, the federal corporate tax rate is a flat percentage of profits. The three-tiered system of rates is shown in the following table:

Taxable Income	Rate of Tax
First $50,000	**15%**
Next $25,000	**25%**
Over $75,000	**34%**

An additional 5 percent tax, up to $11,750, is imposed on corporate taxable income over $100,000 but less than $335,000 (corporations with taxable income of at least $335,000 pay a flat rate of 34 percent).

The regular corporate income tax return is Form 1120. All profit corporations, except those with Subchapter S status (who file Form 1120S) in the past have had to file this return annually by March 15, unless an automatic six-month extension is requested. A new, simplified corporate form has been available since 1985, Form 1120-A (a corporate "short" form, in other words). This two-page return can be filed by all corporations meeting the following requirements:

(1) Gross receipts, total income, and total assets are each less than $500,000
(2) Any dividend income comes from domestic corporations, qualifies for the 70 percent deduction, and is not from debt-financed securities
(3) It has no nonrefundable tax credits other than the general business credit and the credit for prior year minimum tax
(4) The corporation has no ownership in a foreign corporation nor do foreign owners hold 50 percent or more of its own stock
(5) It is not a member of a controlled group of corporations, a member of a group filing a consolidated return, or a personal holding company
(6) It is not in dissolution or liquidation, nor is it filing its final tax return
(7) It is not a Subchapter S corporation or certain other corporations required to file specialized returns, such as farmers cooperatives, political organizations, condominium associations, and real estate investment trusts
(8) It is not subject to liability for interest relating to certain installment sales

Most small corporations will meet all of these tests, and will find their paperwork greatly reduced by using the short form.

Individual Federal Income Tax

Like the State of Indiana, the federal government also taxes corporate profits which are paid out to individual shareholders as dividends. These dividends will be shown on each shareholder's Form 1040 as income and will be taxed at the individual's personal income tax rate.

To escape the double taxation referred to above, you may want to retain the balance of the profits in the corporation so long as you do not exceed the ceiling on accumulated earnings. There are many other ways of taking money out of the corporation tax-free, some of which will be discussed below. If your corporation is very profitable or is overcapitalized in the beginning, however, you may eventually have no choice but to distribute a substantial part of the profits as dividends and pay taxes owed. Otherwise, you will be subject to the IRS "accumulated earnings penalty" already referred to.

Another alternative which avoids double taxation and is often advisable for small, closely held corporations that must pay large dividends regularly is the formation of a Subchapter S corporation (see Chapter 8).

Tax Implications of Employee Compensation and Other Benefits

Salaries

The corporation may deduct on its corporate income tax return as ordinary expenses all amounts paid to employees as salaries. Such salaries must be reasonable and paid for actual services rendered to the corporation.

In this regard, putting family members on the payroll helps to keep income of your business within the family. If family members who draw a salary are not performing duties commensurate with their pay, however, you may have to answer to the IRS. The tax code permits deductions only for "reasonable compensation." This requirement prevents corporations from passing unreasonably large sums of tax-free money to its employee(s).[3] The IRS disallows inflated salaries to be deducted, treating the excess instead as disguised dividends.

It will be up to you to prove that the amount of salary of each employee is "reasonable" in terms of duties, qualifications, and skills of the employee, the complexity of the work performed, the size and profitability of your business, the standard of living in your locality, and the salaries of similar employees in similar businesses.

The IRS also considers the relation of the salary of the owner-employee to other key employees; the larger the salary of other key employees, the larger the salary that can be justified for an owner working full time for the business. In general, more sizeable salaries can also be justified for persons who perform multiple executive roles and for those who head highly profitable companies. For such an owner who is by and large responsible for the success of the business, a salary which is 50 percent of pretax profits is not unusual.

Somewhere down the road, if you have a very profitable corporation and plan to increase your and other key employees' salaries drastically, you will need to exercise prudence and care. Salaries should be set early in the year by the board of directors and should be tied directly to individual performance and productivity. You may well be able to justify paying yourself a salary of, say, $500,000 or even more a year, given your investment of time and money in the business, but be prepared to argue your case.

The IRS often routinely challenges large salaries of one-owner and other closely held or family-run corporations, but its rulings are frequently reversed by the Tax Courts. Judges have ruled $1 million to be reasonable compensation in some cases, but $70 thousand too much in others.

---

3   The employee is taxed on the salary at his or her individual tax rate, of course, but the corporation can write off the entire amount of salaries as a tax deduction. Dividends paid out are likewise taxed to the individual at personal income tax rates, but *cannot* at present be deducted by the corporation as a business expense. In other words, since dividends come out of after-tax earnings, they prove much more costly to the corporation.

In order to help build a case in justifying your salary, you should keep a log of all your business meetings and other professional activities. You might also want to maintain a clipping file of help-wanted advertisements for positions similar to yours which specify a salary. Growth Resources Inc., a Peabody, Mass. company which publishes an annual executive compensation report based on a poll of small and medium-sized companies, is another good source of comparative salary data.

Geneva Cos., a financial-services concern in Irvine, California, has studied 2,500 closely held corporations' compensation by industry group. This data reveals a current median compensation for small business owners of $205,200 in businesses with annual revenue between $1 million and $100,000 million. Most highly paid were the owners of primary metal industries ($340,800 a year), while owners of garden and building materials supplies ranked last, with an average compensation of $153,600. "Compensation" in this survey included salary *and* benefits; salary itself amounted to approximately 78 percent of compensation[4].

Another possible move is to approve a resolution at a directors' meeting and record it in the minutes covering the contingency of an IRS challenge. The resolution would state that in the event the IRS rules officer salaries to be excessive, the officers

in question can pay back the excess amount to the corporation; further, that the amount returned will be treated as a loan to the employees, for tax purposes.

When you are paying yourself such a sizeable salary as to need to consider such techniques, then expert legal counsel would, of course, be advisable. It is also permissable to take a larger salary in more profitable years to make up for a smaller salary in poorer years, but, again, the corporate minutes should state that the salary for a particular year in question is above or below average, due to the financial state of the business.

In general, you should avoid paying large lump-sum bonuses at the end of the year to yourself or other employees. Such bonuses look suspiciously like dividends to the IRS and may be treated as such for tax purposes, since they are paid after the company's earnings for the year are already known. In all tax matters, remember that the success of your claims before the IRS will depend primarily upon the degree of formality you have exercised in your business dealings and the reasonableness of your actions.

Tax-free Pension and Profit-sharing Plans
There are two basic types of pension plans available for businesses, (1) defined contribution plans and (2) defined benefit

---

4   This survey was done some 8 years ago and has not been updated. We have consequently revised each of the salary figures from the original survey upwards by 20 percent.

plans.[5] The former is much simpler to administer, because it limits the amount of actual contributions to a set dollar amount or a percentage of earnings. Under the 1982 Tax Act, a corporation can in post-1982 years make tax-free payments to a defined contribution fund up to the lesser of (a) 25 percent of each employee's annual compensation or (b) $30,000.[6] The amount of money available to the employee during retirement under this arrangement will depend entirely upon the return on pension fund investments.

The second type of pension plan, the defined benefit plan, is more complicated to administer because it pays the retiree a specified amount during retirement. The actual dollar amount of contributions permitted each year can only be determined by an actuary. The 1982 Tax Act permits corporations in post-1982 years to set aside sufficient funds in a defined benefit plan to fund a straight life annuity to the employee on retirement equal to the lesser of (a) $108,963 payout per year[7] or (b) 100 percent of the participant's average compensation for his highest three years. If you choose a defined benefit plan through an insurance company or a bank, it should do all the actuary work and present you with an IRS-approved master plan which you can adopt for your company.

Both types of plans provide tax-deferred benefits to the employee(s), since the funds are allowed to accumulate tax-free until withdrawn, at which time the employee is likely to be in a lower tax bracket. Since these contributions are completely deductible by the corporation as a business expense, they thereby lower the taxable income of the corporation as well. If the corporation is dissolved, the pension funds can be rolled over tax-free into IRA accounts for its employees.

One very important aspect of corporate pension plan set-asides is that such plans cannot discriminate in the owner-employee's favor. If yours is a one-owner corporation, there appears to be no question of discrimination. There are certain precautions that must be taken in such a case of the one employee who is a stockholder.

In addition to being a bona fide plan and meeting the usual requirements, the plan also must provide for coverage of additional employees if and when they are hired. If your company has other employees, you will normally be required to cover them in your benefit plan as well as yourself. You may very well desire to include other employees in your retirement plan as part of your over-all employee compensation package.

There are also certain cases in which employees can be excluded from coverage if you so wish. If your corporation hires "independent contractors," then not only will you not have to cover them in your pension or profit-sharing plans (since they are not

---

5   Legal changes have placed retirement plans for unincorporated businesses more on a par with those available to corporations, but some advantages still remain for corporate plans in the case of defined benefit plans.

6   Down from the maximum allowable contribution per employee of $45,475 in 1982.

7   Down from $136,425 in 1982.

considered employees), but you will also not have to withhold taxes from their salary or pay their Social Security deductions. Part-time employees (who work less than 1,000 hours a year) and those under the age of 21 can generally also be excluded from coverage. If you do wish to set up a corporate pension fund, particularly of the defined benefit type, you may need to see a tax consultant in order to insure favorable tax treatment and legality of this and other corporate perks for employees.

Another angle that you should be aware of is the fact that you can, in certain circumstances, act as trustee of your own corporate pension plan, enabling you to lend money from the benefit fund to yourself. As long as your company approves, furthermore, any of the participants in its pension or other deferred compensation plans can borrow a portion of their contributions back.

The 1982 Tax Act has set limits on these loans, however, because of past abuses in which certain individuals were borrowing the full amount of their tax-deductible retirement contributions. Under the new provisions of the law, the maximum amount you can borrow is $50,000 or half your vested money in the plan, whichever is less.

You are allowed to borrow up to $10,000, however, even if that is more than half the amount you have vested. A further stipulation is that a loan must be repaid within 5 years, unless it is used to buy, build, or refurbish your principal residence. Terms for such home loans range from ten to 25 years.

SEPs

Another pension option especially attractive for the small business owner merits a separate discussion of its own. Simplified Employee Pensions (SEPs for short) offer a relatively new, hassle-free form of retirement plan for **all** types of businesses, whether corporations, partnerships, sole proprietors, or member-managers of a limited liability company. Unlike other types of corporate pension plans, SEPs entail no administrative expense and no burdensome paper work.

For businesses with very limited resources, SEPs are ideal retirement vehicles because of the ease of setting them up and the benefits they provide, which compare favorably with other types of defined contribution corporate pension plans. They have a $30,000 annual limit or 15 percent of compensation, whichever is less. They offer flexible funding. They also offer the advantage of being integratable with Social Security. Most importantly, you do not have to contribute to the plan in those years you can't or choose not to do so.

SEPs for the Masses

The P. Gaines Co. publishes a book about SEPs, **Five Easy Steps to Setting Up an IRS-Approved Retirement Plan for Your Small Business (Incorporated or Unincorporated), With Forms.** *Its easy-to-read text, laced with humorous illustrations, explains how any business that is even modestly profitable can establish a SEP immediately. It walks the reader through the five steps for setting up a SEP and includes all needed forms in a tear-out format. See the order form in the back of this book.*

Medical Reimbursement Plans

Corporate employees, their spouses, and dependents can also be covered with a medical reimbursement plan which pays the cost of medical expenses and drugs. All such corporate medical reimbursements are tax-deductible by the corporation as an ordinary business expense and are passed tax-free to the individuals receiving them.[8] Although referred to as "reimbursement plans" by the IRS, your corporation can pay your medical bills and that of your family directly instead of reimbursing you afterward.

In a small or one-owner corporation, there is no reason why your corporation should not pay 100 percent of your and your family's medical expenses not covered by other insurance, provided there are sufficient funds to do so. Again, be sure to consult a tax adviser who specializes in this area to assure favorable tax treatment of the plan. In a larger corporation, it may be necessary to set a ceiling on the actual dollar amount paid out per employee each year.

A model medical reimbursement plan which you may adopt for use by your corporation is included in Appendix E. *This model plan provides for the payment of all medical bills, including premiums for accident and health insurance.*[9]

This coverage, like that of medical and dental expenses and drugs, may be extended to the spouses and dependents as well as the employees themselves. Accident and health insurance coverage does *not* have to be part of a "group plan" such as those offered by Blue Cross. You can choose your own individual plan and have the corporation pay for it.

Life Insurance

Other employee benefits which are tax-free to the individual and tax-deductible to the corporation include life and disability insurance and workers' compensation insurance. "Free" life insurance purchased by the corporation for its employees is limited to one-year renewable term policies of up to $50,000 coverage per employee. Such insurance plans are normally set up for groups of employees, although even a sole owner-employee of a corporation can qualify under IRS guidelines.

---

8   Whereas the corporation can deduct the total amount spent for medical and dental expenses for its employees, the individual taxpayer, as noted in Chapter 1, can deduct only that portion of expenses exceeding 7.5 percent of adjusted gross income.

9   Unincorporated business owners, whether sole proprietors or partnerships, are now allowed to deduct 30 percent of health insurance premiums paid for themselves and their spouses, subject to certain limitations. This deduction increases to 40 percent of annual health insurance premium expenses in 1997, 45 percent in 1998 through 2002, 50 percent in 2003, 60 percent in 2004, 70 percent in 2005, and 80 percent in 2006 and subsequent years. Both medical and dental health insurance premiums may be deducted, as well as long-term care insurance premiums after tax year 1996. If there are other employees of the business besides the owner(s) they, too, must be provided coverage. If an individual owner is eligible to participate in an employer-sponsored plan, his business cannot also have a plan eligible for the deduction.

The face value of the policy can exceed $50,000, but in such cases the IRS requires the individual to pay taxes on the "imputed income" above $50,000. Nor can the company take a tax deduction for the excess amount over $50,000. This taxable income is computed according to the age of the employee and the approximate amount of premium paid per $1,000. The following table from IRS publication 525 summarizes these variables:

Cost per $1,000 of Protection for One Month

Age*	Cost
Under 30	8 cents
30 through 34	9 cents
35 through 39	11 cents
40 through 44	17 cents
45 through 49	29 cents
50 through 54	48 cents
55 through 59	75 cents
60 through 64	$1.17
65 through 69	$2.10
70 and older	$3.76

Age is determined at end of year (December 31).

You figure the cost for each month of coverage by multiplying the number of thousands of dollars of insurance, figured to the nearest tenth, by the cost from the above table. You must prorate the cost from the table if less than a full month of coverage is involved.

For example, you are 54 years old and your employer provides term life insurance coverage for you in the amount of $80,000. Since $50,000 is excludable from your income, you must figure the amount to include in your income of the remaining $30,000 in coverage. The cost per $1,000 of someone 54 years old is 48 cents (from table). Multiply this figure times 30 (the number of thousands of dollars of the excess amount). This figure of $14.40 (48 cents x 30) is the cost of excess insurance for one month. The amount for the year, $172.80 (12 x $14.40) is the figure which you would show on your personal income tax return as income.

You can also set up an insurance program that gives retired employees (including yourself) up to $50,000 per person of tax-deductible insurance. The retiree would be liable for taxes on insurance above $50,000. Furthermore, you can arrange for group life insurance for immediate family members of the corporation's employees.

Disability Insurance

Premiums paid by your corporation for disability insurance coverage are also deductible by the corporation and tax-free to the employee(s). Although the amount of disability insurance an employee can purchase is limited to a percentage of income, usually in the range of 33 to 60 percent,[10] for higher paid executives the premiums per year may amount to several thousand dollars in tax-free "income." Benefits paid under company-financed plans for tem-

---

10   Insurance companies limit benefits to avoid creating a disincentive to return to work.

porary disability (illness or injury) are included in the employee's gross income and are subject to tax.[11] In the case of permanent and total disability, a partial tax exclusion of benefits is allowed. If the premiums for disability insurance are paid by the employee, however, all benefits, whether for temporary or permanent disability, are non-taxable.

Workers' Compensation

Workers' compensation is another form of insurance which is deductible by your corporation. Workers' compensation insurance set by state law covers any claims for bodily injuries or job-related diseases suffered by employees in your business, regardless of fault. This form of insurance is not even available to sole proprietors, but you are entitled to it as the employee of your corporation.[12]

Interest-free and Low-interest Loans

Another benefit which key employees or sole owner-operators of corporations have enjoyed for decades is the interest-free loan.

For interest-free or below market interest loans made or outstanding after June 6, 1984, the following rules apply. Such loans from the employer to the employee or independent contractor will be treated as though the employee or independent contractor received compensation equal to the market rate of interest that would have been due if the money had been borrowed from a conventional source such as a bank. This imputed compensation must be included in the gross income of the borrower; if the borrower itemizes deductions, he can take an offsetting deduction for the imputed interest expense, however. In order to get the interest deduction at present, the loan must be secured by your home. The interest will then be deductible as home equity loan interest, unless you already have the maximum $100,000 of home equity debt.

Such treatment would normally produce a "wash," without taxable income to the employee, unless the loan was used to carry tax-exempt securities (in which case, no interest deduction is permitted). This interest-free loan perk can be made available to executives of a corporation on a discriminatory basis, that is, it does not have to be offered to all employees or even ones of a particular class or group. Such loans can be made for virtually any purpose from buying a home to financing a child's education.

It is important to note that loans under $10,000 are not treated as though an imputed amount of interest were received and then paid back. In other words, a $10,000 de minimis exception allows loans of this size or smaller to be treated in the old conventional way as interest-free and tax-free.

Corporation-shareholder loans also are subject to the $10,000 de minimis excep-

---

11   The "sick pay exclusion" which in the past treated such benefits as tax-free income was repealed by the Tax Reform Act of 1976.

12   A partnership, moreover, cannot deduct premiums paid for workers' compensation on behalf of partners, since partners are not considered employees of the partnership.

tion. For loans in excess of $10,000 in this area, the imputed interest is treated as transferred from the corporation to the shareholder. Thus, the corporation is considered to have paid a dividend includable in the shareholder's income. The shareholder gets an offsetting deduction, however, and the corporation treats as interest income the amount of imputed interest.

The current rate of imputed interest will be set semi-annually by the Treasury Department, based on market conditions. The law does not make clear whether those individuals who have dual roles as shareholders and employees in a corporation are to be treated under the employer-employee rule or the corporation-shareholder rule.

If you have a corporate pension plan, you can also borrow from it, but the rules prohibit no-interest, below market loans.

Section 23-1-22-2 of the Indiana Business Corporation Law authorizes your corporation to make loans to you as an employee, officer, or director *for any purpose*. The loan may be with or without interest, according to the IRS requirements noted above, and may be secured or unsecured, as the board deems appropriate. Such loans offer one attractive way of taking money out of your business for legitimate personal uses.

It is important, of course, to exercise the proper formality in recording all such loans, by signing a promissory note and carrying the loan on the corporate record books under "Accounts Receivable." By following a fixed repayment schedule, you will avoid potential trouble with the IRS on the issue of whether the loan is actually a disguised dividend.

Tax-free Dividends

Dividends paid to you by *any* corporation are fully taxable as ordinary income. By contrast, if the same stock investments were made by your corporation, 70 percent of the total dividends would escape taxes. The limitations on what qualifies for tax-free treatment are spelled out in IRS Publication 542. Basically, all dividends from domestic U.S. stocks qualify for the 70 percent exclusion, except for dividends from a real estate investment trust and dividends from stock held by your corporation for 45 days or less (90 days or less for preferred dividends).

There exist mutual funds for corporations which invest in stocks that pay dividend income qualifying for the 70 percent corporate exclusion from tax. Two such funds are Vanguard Qualified Dividend Portfolio I (minimum investment of $3,000) and Fidelity Qualified Dividend Fund (minimum investment of $50,000).

Naturally, you will want to maximize your passive income earnings through dividends and other sources. One word of caution, however: you do not want to be considered a "personal holding corporation" by the IRS. A personal holding corporation is defined as a company in which 60 percent or more of corporate profits consists of passive income from stocks, bonds, rents, royalties, etc., and less than 40 percent of profits is derived from business operations. If you do not limit your investment income and are deemed a personal

48

holding company, you will be subject to especially heavy punitive taxes.

Other Tax-deductible Benefits and Expenses

The payment of rent, utility, and phone bills for business usage all provide legitimate tax deductions for your corporation. If your office is at home, then you will need to allocate your expenses between business and personal use. If you rent an apartment, it is a good idea to write two checks each month, one business and one personal, for the proportionate part of the total rent in each case. A proportionate percentage of other expenses such as water and electricity can also be deducted by your corporation.[13]

If you have a separate business phone, then the total bill will, of course, be a business expense. If one phone serves both business and personal use, you should keep a log of all long-distance business calls and be sure to pay the full amount of these as a corporate expense. Before 1989, you could deduct the part of the base rate of your residential telephone allocable to business usage. Currently, the base rate of the first telephone into your residence is considered a nondeductible personal living expense, with no business portion allowable.

If you own your home and have an office therein, you can rent office space to the corporation. Rent paid to a stockholder is another area the IRS looks at closely, since excessive rent provides one way for owners of a corporation to take disguised dividends out of the company. Therefore, the amount of rent you charge the corporation should be reasonable in terms of the cost of comparable office space in your vicinity. If you use 10 percent of your home as an office, do not figure the corporate rent as 10 percent of your mortgage and taxes, however. Generally, you will be entitled to a larger deduction than this when you consider what similar office space rents for. You should draw up a formal lease agreement with the corporation, in the event of a future tax audit.

You can also deduct "repairs" to the business portion of your property in the year incurred, while "improvements" must be amortized (deducted over the period of time they are expected to last).

Other tax-free employee benefits that may be provided include free parking, group legal services plans that offer up to $70 in legal services per employee annually (any amount over that would be taxable to the employee), subsidized lunches, and on-site physical fitness facilities. The reimbursement of expenses for operating and maintaining automobiles and other motor vehicles used in your business are deduct-

---

13 A higher percentage may be justified for the business portion in individual cases. Your business may require unusually large expenditures for electricity and water if you are a professional photographer or a beautician, for example.

ible either on a per-mile or actual cost basis.

The depreciation of business equipment such as cars and computers is another form of tax-free benefit. An especially attractive tax break is the current law allowing up to $18,000 of business property to be written off in the first year that it is placed in service (instead of depreciated).[14] Special rules concerning this write-off apply to cars.

Your corporation can also pay and deduct up to $5,000 as a tax-free death benefit to the beneficiary of any employee, including yourself.

In 1996, educational expenses up to $5,250 per employee are also deductible by the corporation and tax-free to the recipient. Your company could pay for tuition, books, supplies, and other education-related equipment for either work-related or non-job-related courses taken by employees (but not for those graduate courses leading to a degree in law, business, medicine, or other advanced or professional degrees). The eligibility of such a program depends on (1) its being in written form, (2) the giving of reasonable notice of the plan and its terms and availability to all eligible employees, and (3) its not being discriminatory in favor of certain officers, shareholders, or key employees, or spouses or dependents of such individuals.

There is also a stringent restriction on the amount of benefits available to shareholders of the corporation: No more than 5 percent of the benefits paid or incurred by the employer during the year can go to that group of individuals (and their dependents) each of whom holds more than a 5 percent stock interest in the company.

Other tax-free benefits include the cost of convention travel as well as food, lodging, and related expenses incurred by employees attending meetings to increase business know-how and to upgrade skills. Foreign conventions, with several exceptions, are generally not deductible, although travel abroad for business purposes *is* deductible.

Your corporation can also give you and other employees a discount on goods and services. The Tax Reform Act of 1984 placed a limit on the amount of such tax-free discounts. The discount is now limited to your "gross profit percentage." If your profit margin averages 30 percent, then any discount over this percentage will be taxable. The discount must be available to all employees on a non-discriminatory basis. You can also offer up to a 20 percent tax-free discount on services.

Finally, a corporation, unlike a sole proprietorship or a partnership, can deduct charitable contributions up to 10 percent of its taxable income. Contributions in excess of this limitation can be carried over and deducted for up to five succeeding years, subject to certain limitations. Your corporation thus gives you the opportunity, unavailable to the sole proprietor or partnership, to support a charity or cause with tax-deductible business dollars.

---

14 This write-off amount is scheduled to be gradually raised each year until it reaches a $25,000 annual deduction in the year 2003 and beyond.

Chapter 5. FORMING YOUR OWN INDIANA CORPORATION

If you have carefully read the preceding chapters and have decided that you are one of the many individuals who can benefit from the corporate form of business, you are now ready to learn about the procedure for setting up your own for-profit Indiana corporation.[1]

Corporate Name

The first step in organizing your profit corporation is the choice of a name for your business which you like and which complies with state law. The Indiana statutes specify that your corporate name must contain either the word "corporation," "incorporated," "company," or "limited," or an abbreviation of one of these words ("corp.," "inc.," "co.," or "ltd."), or words or abbreviations of like import in another language. Also, the name you select must be "distinguishable" from (1) that of other profit corporations (domestic or foreign) authorized to do business in Indiana; (2) that of not for profit corporations incorporated or authorized to transact business in Indiana; (3) that of limited liability companies or limited liability partnerships

authorized to do business in Indiana; (4) that of names registered or reserved but not yet in use (discussed below).

If you are presently running a business in the state as a sole proprietor or partner, you can use the same business name for your corporation as you presently have by just adding "Inc.," provided that another corporation is not now operating in Indiana under the same name. Even if the name you choose for your corporation is your own name, you still may not be able to use it if it turns out that someone is already doing business in Indiana under that name, unless you modify it in some way in order to clearly distinguish your business name from the other person's.

Just because your name happens to be McDonald, don't imagine that you can open a McDonald's Restaurant in South Bend. But perhaps a McDonald's Dry Cleaners will work, provided one is not already registered with the Indiana Secretary of State.

The one exception to this rule is that a proposed corporation name will be accepted even if it is not distinguishable from the name of an existing corporation,

---

1   If you are considering forming a Professional Corporation as a doctor, dentist, engineer, etc., we suggest that you read this chapter first, then Chapter 6, which deals specifically with the Indiana Professional Corporation. Also see Chapter 7, regarding the Indiana not for profit corporation.

provided that the existing corporation gives its consent to the use of its name. The consent must be in writing and signed by a current officer of the existing corporation. This consent must be submitted when Articles of Incorporation, or an Application for a Certificate of Authority (in the case of a foreign corporation), or an amendment to change the name of a corporation is submitted to the Secretary of State. If consent cannot be obtained because the corporation has gone out of business, a returned (unopened) certified letter seeking consent from the existing corporation will be accepted as granting permission for use of the name.

The Name's The Thing

The P. Gaines Co. publishes a helpful and widely reviewed book on selecting names for use in commerce: **Naming Your Business and Its Products and Services: How to Create Effective Trade Names, Trademarks, and Service Marks to Attract Customers, Protect Your Good Will and Reputation, and Stay Out of Court!** *Every business, whether a corporation, a partnership, a sole proprietorship, or a limited liability company needs to have a business name under which it conducts its affairs. Need we point out that it is important that such a name be legal, from the standpoint of trademark law, as well as catchy. This guide will show you how to have the best of both worlds. See the order form in the back of this book.*

In the event you do incorporate, it is important to realize that even though the business name you select for your company is approved by the Indiana Secretary of State for incorporation purposes, this is no guarantee of the legality of the use of the name from the standpoint of trademark law. You may still be sued by an incorporated or unincorporated company in Indiana or another state for trademark infringement if the name chosen is the same as, or deceptively similar to, that of the other company's.

The use of your family surname as your business name, furthermore, is often the worst possible choice, for several reasons. *Naming Your Business and Its Products and Services* fully explains these and other significant issues in the business name selection process, whether that of a trade name, trademark, or service mark.

In addition, your company name cannot falsely imply professional affiliation or mislead in other ways. "Architect," "Landscape Architect," "Engineer," "Surveyor," and derivatives, for example, may only be used by Professional Corporations that have complied with the requirements of the state board of registration of that profession as well as all applicable statutory provisions. Your company name cannot falsely imply government affiliation nor suggest the conduct of business as a bank or a savings and loan or an insurance company.

The name of the corporation need not be in the English language, provided that it is written in English letters or Arabic or Roman numerals.

Since you have to include the name of your corporation in the Articles of Incorporation which you file with the Secretary of State, you may want to reserve the name you have decided on in advance. You can submit to the Secretary of State a written application requesting the use of a specified name as the name of your corporation (along with a twenty-dollar filing fee). A copy of a form which you may use to reserve a corporate name is included in the back of this book in Appendix E. If the name specified in your application is available, you will be given the exclusive right to use it as the name of your corporation for a period of one hundred and twenty days (at the expiration of the 120-day period, you may renew the reservation and continue to renew it as many times as you wish).

If you are in a hurry to incorporate, the quickest procedure is to ask for a telephone confirmation of the availability of a particular name by calling (317) 232-6576. Someone will check immediately while you wait to see if the name you want is available. Although a telephone check is a reliable indication in most cases, it does not absolutely guarantee the availability of a particular name which is cleared in this fashion. The Corporation Division reserves the right to make its final decision on the matter when a name reservation request has been approved or Articles of Incorporation have been filed.

As a necessary precaution, do not have business stationery or customized stock certificates printed or make other commitments to a name until the Articles of Incorporation have been filed, approved, and returned to you.

To save time, it may be a good idea to either reserve your name in advance or at least have a preliminary name check via phone. Otherwise, your Articles will be returned to you unfiled if the name you have chosen has already been taken, and you will have to refile again under another name . . . and again . . . and again, until you hit on a name that isn't currently being used. A little foresight and advance planning will eliminate these potential delays.

The Articles of Incorporation

In order to obtain corporate status, you will now need to fill out and mail to the Secretary of State one original copy and two photocopies of your Articles of Incorporation, Form 4159. This form is simple to complete in most cases. A copy of this form is available in Appendix A in the back of this book. If the form has already been removed or you have a library edition of this book whose forms are not of the tear-out variety, additional copies can be obtained by writing the Indiana Secretary of State, 302 W. Washington Street, Room E018, Indianapolis, Indiana 46204; telephone (317) 232-6576. You can also request copies of this form by dialing Fax Back (800) 726-8000 (inside Indiana only) and following instructions. When completing the form, which must be filled out in the English language, you should either type or print clearly in black ink all information.

Following on pages 55 and 56 is a sample Articles of Incorporation. Articles of Incorporation *must* furnish only four items of information: (1) the corporate name and address; (2) the name and Indiana street address of the corporation's registered office and the name of the registered agent at that office; (3) the number of authorized shares of stock; (4) the name and address and signatures of each incorporator.

In the first box, you are asked to check whether the business you are incorporating is to be a regular for-profit corporation formed under the Indiana Business Corporation Law or a Professional Corporation organized under the Professional Corporation Act of 1983. If the latter, be sure to read Chapter 6 on the Indiana Professional Corporation immediately after finishing this chapter.

In the next box appears **Article I**, concerning the name of the corporation, which we have already discussed. Be sure to consult our publication, *Naming Your Business and Its Products and Services*, before making your final name selection, to alert you to the legal pitfalls of a poorly chosen moniker and the potential rewards of an effective and legally defensible commercial name (see the order form in the back of this book for details on this publication). Assuming you have found an available name to your liking which is legally sound and distinctive, you can fill it in here. In this same box, you are also asked to fill in the address of the principal office of the corporation.

Article II asks for information about the registered office and the registered agent of the corporation. The purpose of this information is to provide for public record a legal mailing address and contact person to receive corporate mailings from the Secretary of State, as well as legal documents (summons, subpoenas) in connection with any lawsuits that might arise against the corporation. The registered agent must be a resident of Indiana and would ordinarily be one of the corporate directors. The registered office must be located in Indiana, and its street address given (post office box alone not acceptable). In theory, you could authorize anyone residing in Indiana to act as your registered agent, such as an attorney or a friend.[2]

If you are the sole owner-operator of the proposed corporation, you can simply fill in your own name as registered agent and your business address as the address of the registered office. Any changes in the address of the registered office or the name of the registered agent at a later date must be reported to the Secretary of State. Such changes do not require amendment of the Articles of Incorporation or the payment of any filing fee and do not necessitate shareholder or director approval. A written statement mailed to the Secretary of State, indicating the former registered office and agent and the new office and agent and the new agent's agreement to serve in this capacity is sufficient.

Article III concerns the issue of stock. According to our recommendation in Chapter 2, you would authorize stock of common class, no-par value, with a large number of authorized shares (3,000, for instance). You

---

2   There are corporations which provide registered offices and registered agents for other corporations, but these companies are normally used as agents by large corporations with offices in a number of states or "foreign" corporations doing business in Indiana.

ARTICLES OF INCORPORATION

State Form 4159 (R10 / 8-95)
Approved by State Board of Accounts 1995

SUE ANNE GILROY
SECRETARY OF STATE
CORPORATIONS DIVISION
302 W. Washington St., **Rm. E018**
Indianapolis, IN 46204
Telephone: (317) 232-6576

STRUCTIONS: *Use 8 1/2" x 11" white paper for inserts.*
Present original and two (2) copies to address in upper right corner of this form.
Please TYPE or PRINT.
Upon completion of filing, the Secretary of State will issue a receipt.

Indiana Code 23-1-21-2
FILING FEE: $90.00

ARTICLES OF INCORPORATION

The undersigned, desiring to form a corporation *(hereinafter referred to as "Corporation")* pursuant to the provisions of:

☒ ﬁndiana Business Corporation Law

☐ Indiana Professional Corporation Act 1983, Indiana Code 23-1.5-1-1, *et seq.* *(Professional corporations must include Certificate of Registration.)*

As amended, executes the following Articles of Incorporation:

ARTICLE I - NAME AND PRINCIPAL OFFICE

me of Corporation *(the name must include the word "Corporation", "Incorporated", "Limited", "Company" or an abbreviation thereof.)*

WANDA GOLD ENTERPRISES, INC.

Principal Office: The address of the principal office of the Corporation is:

st office address	City	State	ZIP code
1829 Moose Ave	Indianapolis	IN	46236

ARTICLE II - REGISTERED OFFICE AND AGENT

Registered Agent: The name and street address of the Corporation's Registered Agent and Registered Office for service of process are:

me of Registered Agent

Wanda Gold

dress of Registered Office *(street or building)*	City	Indiana	ZIP code
1829 Moose Ave	Indianapolis		46236

ARTICLE III - AUTHORIZED SHARES

Number of shares the Corporation is authorized to issue: 3,000 common no-par value

If there is more than one class of shares, shares with rights and preferences, list such information as "Exhibit A."

ARTICLE IV - INCORPORATORS
[the name(s) and address(es) of the incorporators of the corporation]

NAME	NUMBER AND STREET OR BUILDING	CITY	STATE	ZIP CODE
Wanda Gold	1829 Moose Ave	Indianapolis	IN	46236

(See attached Additional Article)

In Witness Whereof, the undersigned being all the incorporators of said Corporation execute these Articles of Incorporation and verify, subject to penalties of perjury, that the statements contained herein are true,

this ___16th___ day of _____April_____, 19 _97_ .

gnature	Printed name
Wanda Gold	Wanda Gold
gnature	Printed name
gnature	Printed name

is instrument was prepared by: *(name)*

Wanda Gold

dress *(number, street, city and state)*

1829 Moose Ave, Indianapolis, Indiana	ZIP code 46236

Additional Article:

Wanda Gold Enterprises, Inc. will be run under a so-called "shareholders' agreement," as authorized under Section 23-1-33-1(c) of the Indiana Code. The corporation will dispense with the board of directors. All the duties of the board of directors will be performed by the shareholders, Wanda Gold, Junior Gold, and Giesela Gold.

are only required to indicate the *number* of authorized shares of stock in this section. If you wish to authorize more than one class of shares, shares with rights and preferences, you may do so by listing such information on a separate attachment, "Exhibit A." Consultation with an attorney is highly recommended if you decide to authorize more than one class of shares.

Concerning capitalization of the corporation, we have suggested that the number of shares actually *issued* be smaller than the number authorized. Thus, if you authorized 3,000 shares in Article III, a smaller number of issued shares would often be appropriate (300, for example). In this way, you can later issue additional shares if need be. In the future, you may wish to issue additional shares in order to add more capital to your business. As long as you do not issue more than the original number authorized in your Articles of Incorporation, you will not need to report these transactions to the state.

In incorporation lingo, the "consideration to be received therefor" is the amount of capital you and other stockholders will pay in exchange for shares of stock. This amount does not need to be indicated on the Articles of Incorporation. Any amount of capital in cash, property, accounts receivable, inventories, etc. may be initially put into your business when you incorporate. We do recommend beginning with enough start-up capital in your corporation to take care of foreseeable short-term expenses.

You don't want to overcapitalize your corporation, on the other hand, since you will more quickly reach the ceiling set by the IRS for accumulated earnings. At that point, money paid to stockholders will usually take the form of dividends, subject to the "double tax" discussed previously. This is generally not a concern for firms with $100,000 or less in start-up capital.

An aside: one good way to keep from tying up more capital than necessary when you incorporate is to provide part of the initial seed money in the form of a short-term loan to the corporation. The corporation need not pay you interest on the loan as long as it is truly of short-term duration, say, three months or less. If it turns out that the corporation needs this loan money for an extended period of time to stay afloat, however, you may run into problems with the IRS in later taking this money out of the corporation.[3] To avoid running afoul of the ever-watchful authorities, larger start-up loans for longer periods of time should carry an interest charge at market rates, which is a deductible expense for the corporation.

Regarding the question of "common" v. "preferred" stock, as noted previously, preferred stock is so named because shareholders of this type of stock receive their dividends first, before all other classes of stock, at a fixed rate of return. Common stock is paid after preferred, at a variable rate depending on the current profitability of the corporation. If the corporation is dissolved, preferred stockholders also would

---

3   The IRS may argue that this money is not actually a loan at all but equity capital needed for day-to-day business operations. Therefore, the return of this money would be considered for tax purposes as a dividend and would be taxable to the recipient.

receive preferential treatment over common stockholders in the division of the corporate assets. Many publicly traded corporations listed on the New York and American Stock Exchanges have both preferred and common stock, but most small, privately held corporations have no need to issue preferred stock.

Even certain small corporations may wish at some point to issue two classes of common stock, one voting and the other non-voting, however, as in the case of some family corporations who want to keep control of the corporation within the hands of several (or even one) family member(s), while giving other family members shares of dividend-paying stock. If you decide to have different classes of stock, the rights of each class concerning voting privileges, dividends, and so on will have to be decided and indicated in Article III. Since there are a number of different rights, preferences, and limitations assignable to stock, legal consultation is highly advisable if you wish to have two or more classes of stock.

Article IV requests both the name(s) and address(es) of the incorporator(s) and his/her (their) signature(s), as well as the date of incorporation. At least one incorporator must sign the Articles. Either a residence or business address may be provided for each incorporator listed, consisting of a street number and name, city, and state.

The incorporator(s) may specify various additional points, if desired, on a separate sheet of paper, such as fixing a duration of the corporation other than perpetual, setting a par value for shares of stock, permitting cumulative voting rights, naming the initial directors of the corporation, or running the corporation according to a shareholders' agreement. Since the "life" of a corporation is assumed to be perpetual in Indiana unless stated otherwise, you may specify a fixed period for your corporation in your Articles of Incorporation. Such a fixed-life corporation might be appropriate in the case of a corporation organized for the purpose of conducting a political campaign, for instance. If you wish to give your corporation the right to have cumulative voting (explained in Chapter 2, page 31), this should be specified here also.

Another major area often covered by additional articles is that pertaining to what is generally termed a "close corporation agreement" (Indiana law does make a distinction between this type of corporation and a regular corporation). The main purpose of a close corporation option is to allow the shareholder(s) of a corporation to agree upon provisions regulating any aspect of the internal affairs of the corporation. The running of the corporation under a so-called "shareholders' agreement" (without a board of directors and other formalities) is permitted and may be specified here. Section 23-1-33-1(c) of the Indiana Statutes provides:

A corporation having 50 or fewer shareholders may dispense with the board of directors or limit the authority of the board by describing in its Articles of Incorporation who will perform some or all of the duties of the board of directors.[4] If a corporation elects to dispense with or limit the authority of the

4   Conversely, an Indiana corporation with more than 50 shareholders *must* have a board of directors to govern it.

board of directors, any reference to the board of directors by this article also includes those persons described in the Articles of Incorporation who will perform the duties of the board of directors.

Small or even one-man or one-woman corporations that wish to dispense with much of the formality of larger corporations may wish to adopt a close corporation agreement. In order to customize the management of the corporation according to their particular needs and limitations, the elimination of the board of directors is frequently a necessity in one-person corporations.

It may be a good idea to maintain a minimum of formality by having traditional offices—that of a president and a secretary-treasurer at least—even if the same person holds both positions. Those completely informal corporations which dispense with both corporate officers and directors by means of a shareholders' agreement may encounter difficulties in getting bank loans, dealing with the IRS, and so on. If yours will be a one-person corporation without a board of directors, your Articles of Incorporation should specify that you alone will perform the duties normally carried out by the board and that you will assume the functions of chief executive officer (president) as well as the administrative and financial roles of secretary-treasurer.

The placing of restrictions upon the transfer of stock to outsiders in order to maintain corporate control by a particular shareholder or group of shareholders is also allowed. See Appendix E for a list of the various options available under a close corporation agreement.

The three completed copies of the Articles of Incorporation (one original, two photocopies) are filed with the Secretary of State's address, shown in the upper right-hand corner of the form), along with the appropriate fee.

All Indiana for-profit corporations pay a standard filing fee of $90.00.

You may phone (317) 232-6576 regarding any questions you have about the filing procedure. Payment must be made in the exact amount due and in the form of a personal check, money order, cashier's check, certified check, or an Indiana attorney's check.

After three copies of the Articles of Incorporation have been correctly filed with the Secretary of State, the Clerk of the Secretary of State's office will return a photocopy to you, stamped, for inclusion in your corporate records. Your corporation's existence officially begins on the filing date.

Transferring Assets and Liabilities to Your New Corporation

When you are ready to start business as a corporation, if you are beginning from scratch, you will simply turn over the assets which you are offering to the corporation as start-up capital in exchange for stock. The actual transfer procedure will be discussed below under "Issuing Shares of Stock."

If you already have a going business (sole proprietorship or partnership), the transfer will be a bit more complicated, since you have the option of transferring liabilities as well as assets. Legal counsel is advisable to assure the best arrangement tax-wise in your individual circumstances.

Generally speaking, the total amount of liabilities transferred (accounts payable is one type of liability, for example) should not exceed the total amount of assets transferred (accounts receivable, inventories, etc.). Since the individual is personally relieved of his liabilities when he forms a corporation and transfers the debts to it, the amount of the net debt assumed by the company is considered a taxable benefit. The IRS will thus regard the excess of liabilities over assets as a cash payment which is taxable to the individual.

To be on the safe side, you can always balance your assets and liabilities by donating some personal assets to the corporation, such as a typewriter, a computer, a file cabinet, a desk, and so on. Of course, if the assets transferred are greater than the liabilities, there is no problem—only the reverse imbalance will result in punitive taxes. If you transfer the entire business to the corporation, including inventory, capital assets, accounts payable and receivable, the IRS will not tax the uncollected receivables as long as you meet one test. You have to receive control of at least 80 percent of the new corporation (including a minimum of 80 percent of voting stock as well as 80 percent of non-voting stock, if applicable).

In Chapter 1, the possibility of taking back only a portion of the value of your appraised business in stock was mentioned. By receiving only $40,000 in stock in partial payment for a business worth, say, $200,000, the balance of $160,000 is treated as a loan from you to the corporation. The corporation consequently issues you a note for $160,000 and pays you back this sum, plus interest, over the term of years you specify in the note. Such an arrangement has the decided advantage of producing mostly tax-free income to you—only the *interest portion* will be taxable. The rest will be treated by the IRS as a return of principal, which is nontaxable.

You also have the option of shutting down your sole proprietorship or partnership, so that you commence business as a corporation on a fresh basis. It may take several months or more to wind down your old business, but you need not wait until this process is totally completed before starting your corporation. Just be sure to keep business records of the proprietorship or partnership separate from those of the corporation, for both tax and legal purposes.

You will also want to notify creditors in writing of the dissolution of the prior business and of the existence of the new corporation. This can be accomplished with a form letter which might accompany your regular business advertisements.

Ordering Corporate Records Book, Seal and Stock Certificates

The Indiana Business Corporation Law requires that every Indiana corporation keep the following records:

• minutes of the meetings and other records of actions of its shareholders;
• minutes of the meetings and other records of actions of its board of directors;
• a record of shareholders, giving the names and addresses of all shareholders, the number, class, and series of shares held by each, and the dates when they became shareholders of record;
• a copy of the bylaws and amendments of the corporation;
• the Articles of Incorporation and amendments, if any;
• "appropriate" accounting records;
• financial statements;
• a list of directors and officers;
• a copy of its annual report.

Records

The P. Gaines Co. offers a reasonably priced and attractive Black Beauty Corporate Outfit which includes a custom engraved seal, 20 custom printed stock certificates, 50 blank sheets of rag content 20-lb. bond Minute Paper as well as a binder for minutes, corporate bylaws, and stock records. Please refer to the back of this book for additional information about this individually customized corporate outfit and an order form.

Indiana law does not require you to have a corporate seal, but many corporations do use one. You may be asked for the seal imprint on formal agreements such as the application for the corporate bank accounts, bank loan papers, and lease agreements. A seal can be ordered from most stationery stores at a cost of approximately $20 to $25. The corporate kit advertised in the back of this book also contains a corporate seal. The corporate seal is circular and contains the name of the corporation exactly as filed with the Secretary of State, the name of the state (Indiana), the words "Corporate SEAL," and the year of incorporation.

While the Indiana statutes no longer require that certificates signed by officials of the corporation must represent shares of stock of Indiana for-profit corporations, we do recommend their use as an effective means of organizing the corporation. The certificate is simply a concrete representation of one's capital holdings in a corporation. A certificate may be used to represent more than one share of stock. Each certificate shall state on its face:

1. The name of the issuing corporation
2. That the corporation is organized under the laws of the state of Indiana
3. The name of the person to whom issued
4. The number of shares represented by the certificate
5. If the shares of the corporation are classified, the designation of the class of shares, and the designation of the series, if any, which such certificate represents
6. If the corporation is authorized to issue different classes of shares or different series within a class, the designations, relative rights, preferences and limitations of the shares of each class or series of shares authorized to be issued (and the authority of the board of directors to determine variations for future series), which shall be set forth on the front or back of the certificate. Alternately, each certificate

may state conspicuously on its front or back that the corporation will furnish to a shareholder all such information upon request in writing and without charge

7. Each share certificate must be signed (either manually or in facsimile) by at least two officers (or the sole officer, if the corporation has only one officer) designated in the bylaws or by the board of directors

8. Each share certificate may bear the corporate seal or its facsimile

9. If the person who signed (either manually or in facsimile) a share certificate no longer holds office when the certificate is issued, the certificate is nevertheless valid

It is standard practice for corporations to imprint their stock certificates with their corporate seal. Stock certificates may be purchased from many of the larger stationery stores. The Black Beauty Corporate Outfit which we offer contains 20 attractive certificates which are custom printed with the corporate name, state, and officers' titles.

Preorganization Subscription Agreement

If you are a one-man band, then a subscription agreement will not be necessary. If other shareholders will be involved in setting up the corporation, however, you may wish to have them sign a "preorganization subscription agreement." This agreement is legally binding in the state of Indiana, provided that it is in writing and signed by the subscriber. A subscription for shares of a corporation to be organized is irrevocable for a period of six months unless the subscription agreement provides a longer or shorter period, or unless all of the sub-scribers consent to the revocation of the subscription.

If a preorganization subscription agreement does not spell out the dates, amount, and other terms of payment for shares, then, according to the Business Corporation Law, the board of directors after incorporation can decide the terms. Once Articles of Incorporation are filed with the Secretary of State, all subscribers for shares shall be deemed to be shareholders of the corporation, and the corporation shall have the right to enforce such subscriptions in its name. The board of directors determines when subscriptions for shares are to be paid (normally immediately following the first board of directors meeting). The call for payment must be uniform for all the shareholders of the same class.

In the case of default, the corporation may proceed to collect the amount due in the same manner as any debt owed to the corporation. It may also rescind the subscription, sell the shares to a third party if the debt remains unpaid more than 20 days after the corporation sends written demand for payment to the subscriber, and sue the defaulter for breach of contract.

A sample subscription agreement follows hereafter. See Appendix E for a copy of this agreement which you can adopt for your own corporation. If you have more subscribers than you can fit on one sheet, you can make as many additional copies of this form as necessary.

PREORGANIZATION SUBSCRIPTION AGREEMENT

We, the undersigned, severally subscribe to the number of shares set opposite our respective names of capital stock of a proposed corporation, to be known as __Wanda GOLD Enterprises, Inc.__ or by any other name that the incorporators may select, and to be incorporated in the State of Indiana. We agree to pay the sum of $____40____ per each share subscribed.

This subscription shall not be binding on the undersigned unless subscriptions in the aggregate amount of $___16,000_____ for shares of said corporation have been procured on or before the __14__ day of ____April_____, 19 _97_ .

All subscriptions hereto shall be payable at such time or times as the board of directors of said corporation may determine and shall be paid in cash, except as hereinafter indicated. (If any of the subscriptions are to be paid by transferring property to the corporation, a description of the property shall be attached hereto.)

Date	Name and Address	Number of Shares	Amount Subscribed
-12-97	Wanda Gold 1829 Moose Ave Indianapolis, IN 46236	200	$8,000.00
/13/97	Junior Gold 912 Virtue Blvd Indianapolis, IN 46220	100	4,000
-13-97	Gizzila Gold 814 Persimmon Lane Indianapolis, Indiana 46208	100	$4,000.00

Preparing the Bylaws

You are now ready to prepare the bylaws for your corporation, which may contain any provision for the regulation or management of the affairs of the corporation that is not inconsistent with law or the Articles of Incorporation. The initial bylaws of a corporation shall be adopted by its incorporator(s) or its board of directors. Only the board of directors has the power to amend or repeal the bylaws or adopt new bylaws, unless power to do so is reserved exclusively to the shareholders by the Articles of Incorporation. (Those small corporations that dispense with the board of directors under §23-1-33-1(c) of the Indiana statutes, as noted above, will of course be governed by the shareholder[s] according to a shareholders' agreement.)

We provide in Appendix B in the back of this book a set of bylaws which you can modify for your corporation's use by filling in the blanks and making minor alterations. If you are having an attorney prepare your incorporation, be sure to ask if he is using a "kit" with standard bylaws; if not, find out why, because you will pay dearly if he or she has to draw up customized bylaws (in most cases, they are unnecessary).

First, indicate the name of your corporation at the top of the page. In Article I, write in the name of the city/village/township (cross out the ones that don't apply) and the county where the principal executive office of the corporation is located.

In Article II, Section 2, indicate the date and time (5th of May at 6 P.M., for example) on which the annual shareholders' meeting is to be held. This will be the same date as the regular directors' meeting (Article III, Section 5). Often this date is set shortly before or after the close of the corporation's fiscal year, so that both the previous year and the coming year's business can be discussed.

If you want your fiscal year to coincide with the calendar year, however (beginning on January 1 and ending on December 31), you will want to hold your annual meeting close to the date on which your corporation is initially organized.

In Article III, Section 2, indicate the number of directors of the corporation. Read through the bylaws to familiarize yourself with the contents. We will assume that your bylaws will be approved at the first shareholders' meeting, although, as noted above, they may be approved by the directors as well.

First Meeting of Shareholders

After the corporation has been organized and the Articles of Incorporation filed with the Secretary of State and returned to you approved, the first meeting of the shareholders can be convened.[5] It is advisable to have each shareholder sign a waiver of notice form (included in Appen-

---

5   As already pointed out, the Indiana statutes provide for the option of a shareholders' agreement whereby the corporate directors may be dispensed with and the business of the corporation conducted entirely by the shareholder(s).

dix C), in order to dispense with formal notice requirements. If there is more than one shareholder, a chairman who will preside at the meeting and a secretary who will keep minutes should be appointed. Minutes of this meeting which may be adopted for most corporations are in Appendix C.

The meeting should be advised that the Articles of Incorporation have been filed and approved. A resolution to approve the Articles and to accept their filing should be made. If a subscription agreement has been used, it should be read and formally approved also.

The chairman informs the shareholders of the number of directors to be elected (if applicable). Nominations are accepted and voted on. The Indiana statutes, as mentioned previously, provide for the option of cumulative voting; if cumulative voting rights are desired (explained on page 31), the Articles of Incorporation must specifically authorize them. As explained in Chapter 2, under cumulative voting procedures the number of votes each shareholder is entitled to is determined by multiplying the number of shares he holds by the number of directors to be elected.

In the case of the three-shareholder corporation of Wanda, Junior, and Giesela Gold, Wanda would have 300 votes and Junior and Giesela 150 votes each, if Wanda holds 100 shares of stock and the other two have 50 shares each and three directors are to be elected under cumulative voting procedures. Each may cast all of his votes for one nominee or divide them among several candidates in any proportion desired. The purpose of cumulative voting

is to give minority shareholders greater voting power and representation than would otherwise be the case.

In the absence of cumulative voting, directors are elected by a plurality of the votes cast. After the election of directors, the corporate bylaws are presented for approval, if the initial bylaws are to be approved by the shareholders. A majority of the voting power represented by the shareholders will constitute approval. After the meeting of shareholders is adjourned, the directors hold their first meeting (assuming that your corporation will have directors).

First Meeting of the Board of Directors

The purpose of the first meeting of the board of directors is to elect officers, adopt the corporate seal and stock certificates, establish a fiscal year, decide on a bank or banks where the corporation will maintain accounts, and to make other types of resolutions. In the back of the book in Appendix D, you will find a set of corporate minutes which may be adopted for the first meeting of the board of directors. You may fill in the blanks with the pertinent information for your corporation and neatly cross out any resolutions that are not applicable to you.

We will go step by step through the first meeting of the board of directors and the preparation of the minutes of the meeting. First, you may tear out the "Waiver of Notice," which is the first form in Appendix D, and fill in the blanks, indicating the date, time, and place of the meeting and have all the directors sign it.

One of the directors is to be chosen chairman and to preside, while another director should be selected to act as secretary. The secretary will complete the first page of the minutes by filling in the time, place, and date of the meeting and the names of the directors present as well as any absentees. The names of the chairman and the secretary are to be shown in the spaces provided.

The meeting should be advised of the filing of the Articles of Incorporation and their approval by the Secretary of State. The filing date should be recorded in the appropriate place in the minutes. The meeting thereafter acknowledges the initial adoption of the bylaws by the shareholders (if the Articles of Incorporation so provide).

An election of officers should be conducted. When completed, the permanent secretary and president will replace the temporary ones appointed previously. The names of the officers elect are shown in the spaces provided in the minutes. As discussed in Chapter 2 under "Officers," one person may hold more than one or even all the offices, if the Articles or the bylaws so provide.

When the resolution concerning the corporate seal has been read and passed, the secretary should make an impression of the seal in the space provided in the right-hand margin. A resolution to adopt the type of stock certificate to be issued by the corporation follows next.

The location of the principal executive office of the corporation should next be entered in the spaces provided.

The directors must establish a fiscal year for the corporation. It is simplest to have your fiscal year coincide with the calendar year (beginning January 1 and ending December 31). You also have the option of having your fiscal year be another twelve-month period ending on the last day of a month other than December (May 1 to April 30, for example). Another possibility allowed by the IRS is to have your fiscal year end on the same day of the week in the same month each year, for instance, the last Friday in June. In this case, your fiscal year will have 52 weeks during some years and 53 weeks in other years. Since various tax and accounting questions are connected to the establishment of a fiscal year, you may want to consult a tax adviser about this issue. Fill in the information concerning the fiscal year in the minutes.

The choice of a bank or banks for corporate accounts should be made and shown in the designated place. If you wish more than one officer to endorse checks, you should insert a separate resolution to this effect.

A resolution approving your "Medical Care Reimbursement Plan" should be presented and adopted, if you wish your corporation to pay the medical expenses of the employees and their dependents. Be sure to consult with a tax adviser to assure the tax-free status of this and other corporate fringe benefit plans (see the discussion in Chapter 4, under "Medical Reimbursement Plans," page 45). A copy of one type of model plan is included in Appendix E.

The next resolution about compensation of officers requires that the officers' salaries be decided upon and shown in the appropriate blanks.

If you wish to elect Subchapter S treatment for your corporation, then a resolution to this effect should be made and included in the minutes. (See Chapter 8, "The S Corporation"). We have included this optional resolution in the minutes. Cross it out if your corporation does not make this election.

Resolutions are also included in the minutes regarding the qualification of common stock as 1244 stock. The purpose of these resolutions is to allow the stockholders of the corporation the benefit of treating losses from the sale, exchange, or worthlessness of their stock as "ordinary" instead of "capital" losses. Since ordinary losses are generally fully deductible whereas long-term capital losses are only 50 percent deductible, it is advantageous to have your stock treated as 1244 stock.

Resolutions concerning the sale and issuance of capital stock are also normally in order. You may fill in the blank showing the number of shares authorized in the Articles of Incorporation. Shares of stock issued for cash are easily entered in the minutes by indicating in the blanks the number of shares purchased and the price of each share. In the case of shares issued for property, the number of shares exchanged for property and the price per share as well as a description of the property are to be shown in the next resolution.

If you are transferring the assets and liabilities of a going business to the corporation in exchange for stock, then you will need to complete the next two resolutions as well. Technically speaking, even if you are the sole owner of a proprietorship and are transferring this business to the corporation, a "Bill of Sale Agreement" should be executed (see Appendix E for a model of this form). The date of the offer of transfer of business, which details the assets and liabilities of the business being transferred, and the fair market value of the business should be indicated in the appropriate blanks.

Finally, the secretary will need to sign the last page of the minutes. A copy of the waiver of notice, a copy of the prepared minutes, a copy of the Articles of Incorporation, a sample copy of the corporation stock certificate (with the word "SPECIMEN" written across the face), a copy of the bank depository resolution form, and any other applicable forms should be placed in the corporate records book. Stock certificates and stubs may be placed in a separate binder or in a special section of the same binder as the other corporate records. Minutes of future meetings of shareholders and directors and all other documents pertaining to the corporation such as loan agreement forms and other legal papers should be filed with the corporate records upon receipt.

The corporate records book is required by law to be kept at the principal executive office at all times. In the event of an audit by the IRS or a lawsuit, your corporate records may be subject to close scrutiny. No matter how small your corporation, if you do not keep proper records, you may be subject to various legal and tax penalties.

Issuing Shares of Stock

Once the first meeting of the board of directors is concluded, stock certificates can now be issued in exchange for cash or the assets of a going business.

Currently, you do *not* have to register with the Securities Department stock issued by your corporation which is valued at $250,000 or less or is issued to 15 or fewer individuals residing in Indiana. There may be a filing requirement for corporations that do not fit these two categories. Contact the Secretary of State if your stock issuance does not conform to these requirements.

Each share certificate can represent any number of shares of stock, the number of shares to be indicated in the upper right-hand corner of the certificate. In addition, each certificate can be issued to more than one person if desired, in the case of husband and wife or other individuals who wish to hold stock jointly with rights of survivorship or as tenants in common or as tenants by the entireties. A sample stock certificate and instructions for filling it out follow hereafter.

Instructions for Filling out Stock Certificates
First, you may fill out the stub portion of the stock certificates, which is either attached directly to the certificates or separate. The stubs are attached to the cer-

tificates on their sides in this book (see back of book). You may detach stub and certificate by tearing along the dotted lines. Concerning the certificate number at the very top of the stub, you may simply number each certificate consecutively, 1, 2, 3, etc. You will need to be sure that the number shown here matches the number on the face of the certificate. The reason for this is that the stub numbered 1 will be the corporate record of the certificate numbered 1, issued to a particular shareholder. Next, complete the section below by showing the number of shares purchased by the individual, the name and address of the stockholder, and the date of issuance.

You would ordinarily leave the middle section of the stub, "From Whom Transferred," blank. This is used in the case of transfer of the certificate to a new owner.

At the bottom of the stub, you will again indicate the certificate number, the number of shares, and the date of issuance, and have the stockholder sign on the bottom line as proof of receipt.

On the stock certificate proper, indicate the certificate number in the upper left-hand corner and the number of shares represented by the certificate in the upper right-hand corner. Fill in the name of the state in the space under the words "Incorporated Under the Laws of ." The upper middle portion of the certificate has a blank space in which to write the name of the corporation. In the body of the certificate, you may simply fill in the blanks for the owner's name and the number of shares.

In the space for the name of the shareholder, you can, as noted, write in

more than one name. If this is done, you would normally put in brackets after the names the type of joint ownership elected, for example: **Junior and Concha Gold (joint tenants in common)**.

On the right side of the certificate outside the border, you can indicate that your stock issuance conforms with Section 1244 of the Internal Revenue Code for favorable tax treatment, allowing you to deduct corporate losses as an ordinary loss deduction on your personal income tax return (subject to certain limitations). If you choose to have your stock treated as 1244 Stock, you may type the following statement on this portion of the stock certificate:

THESE SHARES ARE ISSUED IN ACCORDANCE WITH SECTION 1244 OF THE INTERNAL REVENUE CODE

An impression of the corporate seal may be made at the bottom of the certificate. The date of issuance should also be shown in the place provided. There is space at the bottom of each certificate to type the names of the president and secretary, after each have signed in the appropriate spot. The Indiana Code states that the share certificates must be signed by at least two officers of the corporation, designated by the bylaws or the board of directors to sign the shares. In the case of a one-officer corporation, the one officer's signature is, of course, sufficient.

Each shareholder is given a completed certificate in exchange for cash or the assets of a going business. Stock issued in exchange for cash should be paid for by personal check so that the shareholder will have proof of payment. It is recommended that receipts for cash payments also be is-

sued by the corporation, showing the amount of money received, the check number, the name of the shareholder and the number of shares purchased, the name of the corporation, and the name of the treasurer, as well as the treasurer's signature.

A duplicate copy of each shareholder's receipt should be kept in the share certificates section of the corporate records book. Regarding stock issued in exchange for the assets of a going business, a copy of the signed and dated Bill of Sale (See Appendix E for this form) will provide documentation of this transaction.

Employer Identification Number

As soon as possible after filing the Articles of Incorporation and selecting a fiscal year for your corporation, you should apply to the IRS for an Employer Identification Number (EIN). You may already have an EIN if you are in business as a sole proprietor. This one won't work, however. You will be required to obtain a new EIN as a corporation.

The form to file is an SS-4, Application for Employer Identification Number. You can phone the IRS and request an SS-4 by mail (see directory of important phone numbers in the back of this book) or perhaps pick one up in person from a local IRS office. It will usually take 3 to 6 weeks after applying to receive your number. It is also possible to receive an EIN quicker by faxing your request to (606) 292-5760 and including your fax number. The IRS will notify you by fax in 3 to 5 working days of your number.

If any forms, such as your application for a corporate bank account, ask for the EIN before it arrives, you can put down "number applied for" with the understanding that you will notify the appropriate authorities immediately upon receipt.

Filing an Assumed Name

Another procedure may apply to some newly formed corporations. Say you incorporate your business under the names of the principals, Unamuno, Grimmelshausen, and Horowitz, Inc. When you are ready to print business stationery, have business signs painted, or run ads about your new company, you may have second thoughts about using such an awkward name, so you decide to call yourselves UGH, Inc. for short. In all such cases, you must file the assumed name by submitting a Certificate of Assumed Business Name to the County Recorder in each county in which the corporation has an office or a place of business.

A copy of this certificate, providing the actual and assumed name of the corporation and its principal office address in Indiana, and bearing the file mark of the County Recorder, must then be filed with the Secretary of State, accompanied by a $30.00 filing fee. Whenever the name

under which you do business is different in some way from the one you originally filed when you incorporated, you must follow this procedure. A fine of up to $1,000 may be imposed on a company that fails to register its assumed name. If you operate under the exact corporate name that you filed under, then it is, of course, not necessary to file an assumed name. [6]

Corporate Changes

The Business Corporation Law permits an incorporated Indiana business to amend its Articles of Incorporation at any time. If you make mistakes of judgment in your original Articles of Incorporation which you later wish to correct, if you wish to change any provision(s) of the original Articles, change the name of the corporation, convert from a regular to a not for profit corporation, or authorize additional shares of stock, change your status to that of a close corporation, and so on, you must notify the Secretary of State of these and similar changes.

Many amendments to the Articles of Incorporation require shareholder approval. See Indiana Code §23-1-38-1, which spells out the various details to be followed in amending the original Articles. Amended Articles of Incorporation must be signed by a current officer of the corporation and accompanied by a filing fee of $30.00. Other changes, such as changing the registered office or agent, require no fee payment.

6   If a foreign corporation wishes to do business in Indiana but finds that its corporate name is not available in this state since another Indiana business is already using it, this foreign corporation has to adopt a fictitious business name. This procedure will not be detailed here, since it will not apply to most users of this book.

Chapter 6. THE INDIANA PROFESSIONAL CORPORATION

This chapter will point out certain general characteristics of professional service corporations and discuss specific Indiana laws governing their formation in this state.

Professional Liability

As noted in Chapter 1, the owner(s)-operator(s) of an Indiana professional service corporation cannot limit personal liability by means of the "corporate veil" like employees of regular corporations. Nevertheless, professionals who incorporate have more protection from liability than a partnership or sole proprietor.

Although the corporate form does not shield you from personal liability as a professional practitioner in the case of your own malpractice, it does limit your liability as a shareholder of the corporation. If your business goes bankrupt, the personal service corporation protects your personal assets from creditors in the same way that a regular corporation does. A professional service corporation may also provide you with a degree of protection from malpractice on the part of your associates (but not from the malpractice of other employees of the corporation who are under your direction or direct control).

Fringe Benefits

Many of the same benefits exist for the professional corporation as for the regular for-profit corporation, such as the deductibility of medical and dental expenses and of premiums paid for medical, disability, and life insurance (up to $50,000 group-term coverage per employee), a $5,000 death benefit, free meals and lodgings furnished for the convenience of the corporation, deductible educational expenses up to $5,250 per employee, employee discounts on goods and services, free parking, group legal services plans, on-site physical fitness facilities, and deductible charitable contributions up to 10 percent of taxable income per year.

Limit on Business Activities

Your professional service corporation cannot engage in any business other than rendering those professional services for which it is licensed by the state and which may be specifically noted in its Articles of Incorporation: accounting services for accounting professionals, architectural or engineering services for architectural or engineering professionals, legal services for attorneys, health care services for health care professionals, land surveying for land surveyors, real estate transactions for real estate professionals, psychology for psychologists, and veterinary services for veterinarians. Of course, clerical and technical employees are exceptions to this rule. Your professional association may employ these types of workers to render services of a non-professional nature.

Your professional service corporation is permitted to own stocks, bonds, mortgages, real estate, and other real or personal property. Section 23-1.5-2-3(c) of the Indiana Code states that "a professional corporation may invest its funds in any type of investment not prohibited by law." We have already pointed out in earlier chapters the tax advantages of corporate v. individual ownership of passive income-producing property in certain instances (only 30% of corporate stock dividends are taxable, for instance).

Tax Dangers

One aspect of the 1982 federal tax act is especially crucial for personal service corporations. This law permits the IRS to "pierce the corporate veil" in those cases where a corporation performs substantially all of its services for one other corporation, partnership, or other business entity (for example, a corporation of doctors who all work exclusively for one hospital). In such instances, the IRS now has the power to reallocate income and deductions from the professional service corporation to the individual owners (to the financial detriment of the individuals!). The best way to avoid this problem as an incorporated profes-

sional is to make sure that your company provides services to more than one client, whether to several hospitals, clinics, or to the public itself. Other devices for assuring the tax-favored status of your professional association can be suggested by a competent legal adviser specializing in this area.

Flat Tax Rate

In the past, professional service corporations enjoyed the same graduated federal corporate tax rates as for-profit corporations. This is no longer the case. Professional service corporations involved in activities or services in the fields of health, law, engineering, architecture, accounting, actuarial science, performing arts, and consulting are now taxed at a flat rate of 34 percent (the lower 15 percent and 25 percent tax brackets are no longer available to these types of corporations).

This does not mean that 34 percent of your personal service corporation's income will be paid out to the IRS each year. Only the *profits*, if any, remaining in the corporation at the end of its tax year will be subject to this flat tax rate. Most personal service corporations accumulate little, or no, profits, however, since their income is largely paid out in deductible salaries, retirement plan contributions, and tax-free fringe benefits. Few personal service corporations will consequently pay substantially more taxes as a result of this tax law change. A tax adviser can help you determine if incorporating your practice will result in an increase in tax liability under your individual circumstances.

Personal service corporations, like regular for-profit corporations, have the option of electing to become S corporations and be taxed at personal federal income tax rates, if this proves advantageous. The major disadvantage of S corporations is that certain fringe benefits are not available to them (See Chapter 8, "The S Corporation").

The procedure whereby you can incorporate your practice is virtually the same as for a regular for-profit corporation. Aspects of incorporation unique to the Professional Corporation will be outlined below. You will want to weigh the advantages and disadvantages of incorporation and may wish to seek the advice of a legal counselor concerning the advisability of such a step in your particular case.

INCORPORATING AS A PROFESSIONAL IN INDIANA

The Indiana Professional Corporation Act authorizes the formation of professional service corporations for the sole purpose of rendering a professional service. "Professional service" includes any professional service which is licensed by the state of Indiana, the U.S. Patent and Trademark Office, or the Internal Revenue Service, including such professional practitioners in Indiana as architects, attorneys, certified or other public accountants, land surveyors, engineers, podiatrists, dentists, pharmacists, real estate professionals, psychologists, nurses, and medical practitioners.

Other Powers of Professional Service Corporations

In addition to rendering professional services, professional service corporations are also granted the power, under the Indiana Professional Corporation Act, to invest their funds in stocks, bonds, real estate, and other forms of investment, as noted above, and to own real or personal property necessary for rendering professional services. How far a professional service corporation may go in making certain types of investments completely unrelated to its professional practices, for example, the purchase of raw land, is unclear but evidently allowed.

Limits on Mergers or Consolidations

A professional corporation organized in Indiana can consolidate or merge with another domestic or foreign corporation only if every shareholder of each corporation is qualified to be a shareholder of the surviving or new corporation. In the case of a merger or consolidation in which the new or surviving corporation would render professional services in Indiana, every shareholder, then, would have to be licensed to render such professional services in this state.

Annual and Biennial Report Requirement

There is an annual report requirement for Indiana professional service corporations to assure that non-professionals do not set up and run professional corporations. Before July 30 of each year, every professional service corporation in the state must file with the Secretary of State a report showing the names and addresses of all shareholders of the corporation and shall certify that all shareholders are duly licensed or otherwise legally authorized in this state to render the same professional service as the corporation. The appropriate form is automatically mailed to each professional service corporation in the state. IMPORTANT NOTE: This annual report is *in addition to* the biennial report that all for-profit corporations, including professional service corporations, must file every other year before the end of the month in which the business was incorporated (see page 37). Indiana Professional Corporations, in essence, must file two reports, one annual and one biennial.

Corporate Organization

The manner of organizing a professional service corporation is basically the same as that of a regular for-profit corporation. A minimum of one incorporator is required, who would be the professional practitioner himself or herself. The Articles of Incorporation for professional service corporations is the same form as that for a general business corporation. See pages 53-59 for basic instructions on filing out this form. The filer must, of course, check the box indicating that the corporation is being organized under the Professional Corporation Act. A copy of the Articles form is included in Appendix A.

Board of Directors

A professional service corporation may be governed in the same manner as a regular for-profit Indiana corporation, either by a board of directors elected by the shareholders and represented by officers elected by the board of directors or under a shareholders' agreement (see above, pages 58-59 for a discussion of operating under a shareholders' agreement). If the corporation is organized on a directorial basis, the directors of the Professional Corporation and all the officers as well (with the exception of the secretary and the treasurer) *must* be licensed to render the specific professional services for which the corporation was formed. [1]

Corporate Name

In completing the Articles, the first item, the corporate name, is subject to the provisions of the general corporation law discussed in Chapter 5. The name selected, that is, must be distinguishable from other names of corporations already doing business in Indiana.

The following provisions, in addition, apply to the business names of professional service corporations in Indiana. (1) The name of a corporation organized as a professional service corporation must contain the words "Professional Services Corporation" or "Professional Corporation" or an abbreviation of these words (ordinarily abbreviated P.S.C. or P.C.). (2) The name may not contain any word or phrase that in-

---

1   The offices of secretary and treasurer may be, but do not have to be, filled by persons who are *not* licensed to render the professional services for which the corporation was organized.

dicates or implies any purpose or power not possessed by corporations organizable under the Professional Corporation Act. (3) The name may not contain any word or phrase that indicates that it is organized for any purpose other than that listed in the Articles of Incorporation. (4) Only a professional corporation in which all shareholders are physicians licensed under IC 25-22.5 may use the term "medical" in its corporate name. A licensing authority may by rule adopt further requirements than these as to the names of professional corporations organized under this Act.

Specific Purpose Clause in Articles

Indiana no longer requires a specific purpose clause in the Articles of a professional service corporation that states the particular professional purpose for which the professional association is being organized. We would recommend attaching another sheet of paper to the Articles form and including a specific purpose clause, however. Unlike other types of profit corporations, an Indiana professional corporation must adhere to one specific professional practice, whether or not it is spelled out in the Articles. For example, the following formula or a similar one may be used, filling in the name of the particular profession in the blank:

PROFESSIONAL CORPORATION: To practice the profession of _____, rendering that type of professional service and services ancillary thereto.

Professional services will be rendered from the following address:

Certificate of Registration

Prior to submitting the Articles of Incorporation in order to set up a Professional Corporation, a certificate of registration must first be obtained. The certificate is filed with the Articles. Each licensed profession in Indiana has a procedure for issuing such a certificate and a specific bureau to which to make application. Contact the appropriate bureau and follow its instructions regarding the issuance of such a certificate for persons in your profession. For information on professional licensing in Indiana, phone 1-800-45STATE.

An accounting professional, for example, will apply to the State Board of Public Accounting, whereas an architect will apply to the Board of Registration for Architects and an engineer to the Board of Registration for Professional Engineers. An attorney will apply to the Indiana Supreme Court and a veterinarian to the Indiana Board of Veterinary Medical Examiners.

Once you submit the required application, the appropriate licensing authority will review it to determine that the directors and shareholders of the proposed corporation are properly licensed in compliance with the law and that the corporation will be organized legally. After this determination is made, with the payment of a registration fee of $25.00, a certificate of registration will be issued.

The certificate of registration must be presented along with the Articles of Incorporation for filing. Once approved by the

Secretary of State, the endorsed certificate of registration and a copy of the Articles will be returned to you.

Filing of Copy of Articles with Bureau

After your professional corporation is organized, you must then file a copy of its Articles of Incorporation with the appropriate regulating authority for your profession. Thereafter, the corporation shall file with the appropriate licensing bureau certified copies of all amendments to its Articles of Incorporation, including Articles of Acceptance and all Articles of Merger.

A Professional Corporation shall notify the Secretary of State and the appropriate licensing bureau of a change in ownership of any of the shares in the Professional Corporation or a change in its business address within 30 days after the date of the change. Notice of change in ownership must contain the names and post office addresses of the transferer shareholder and the transferee shareholder, and notice of change of business address must contain the street address of the old location and the street address of the new location.

Renewal of Certificate of Registration

The certificate of registration must be renewed biennially before January 31 of even numbered years. The holder of the certificate of registration must apply for renewal by submitting to the appropriate licensing bureau a written application upon a form prescribed by the bureau and a fee of $20.

Articles of Acceptance

There exists a procedure whereby corporations organized prior to September 1, 1983, the date when the Indiana Professional Corporation Act first went into effect, can now avail themselves of the rights and privileges of this Professional Corporation Act. They can legally conform to the requirements of the Act through the submission of Articles of Acceptance to the Secretary of State. This procedure is outlined in §23-1.5-4-5 of the Indiana Code.

Stock Division

The Indiana Code (§23-1.5-3-3) provides detailed instructions regarding the disposition of the shares of any shareholder upon his death or disqualification to perform professional services. In essence, the shares of the decedent or disqualified person must either be transferred to a qualified person or purchased or redeemed by the corporation itself to the extent that the corporation has funds which may legally be available for such a purchase. (No purchase of or payment for its own shares may be made at a time when the corporation is insolvent or when the purchase or payment would make it insolvent.) All such transfers of stock ownership of the Professional Corporation, as noted above, require notification of the Secretary of State and the appropriate licensing bureau within 30 days of the date of the change.

Professional Service Corporations Possess the Same Powers and Limitations as Regular Corporations

The powers which regular corporations enjoy and the limitations on regular corporations apply to professional service corporations as well.

77

Chapter 7. THE INDIANA NOT FOR PROFIT CORPORATION

The Indiana Nonprofit Corporation Act of 1991 allows corporations with a number of different purposes to be organized under this Act. All such corporations organized or reorganized under this chapter of the Indiana Code have in common the fact they do not engage in any activities for the profit of their members and that they are organized and conduct their affairs for purposes other than the pecuniary gain of their members. Not for profit corporations traditionally include a broad range of charitable, benevolent, educational, civic, political, religious, social, literary, athletic, and scientific purposes. A wide variety of corporations, from those organized to run political campaigns to those engaged in humanitarian endeavors, may be formed under this section.

In spite of its nonprofit purpose, employees of a not for profit corporation are entitled to draw a reasonable salary for services rendered to the corporation, but neither they nor the directors or members can take earnings out of the corporation in the form of dividends or other personal benefits.

Not for Profit Articles of Incorporation

An Indiana not for profit corporation is similar in certain respects to an Indiana profit corporation but different in others. As in the case of a profit corporation, Articles of Incorporation must be filed with the Secretary of State in order to set up the corporate entity. A copy of the not for profit Articles is included in Appendix E.

Articles of Incorporation of a not for profit corporation shall be executed and filed in triplicate (one original plus two photocopies) and shall set forth:

(**1.a**) The name of the corporation.
(**1.b**) The address of the principal office.
(**2**) The *specific* purpose or purposes for which the corporation is organized. provided you want to obtain tax-exempt status from the IRS and the state of Indiana. Otherwise, you have the option of using a blanket purpose clause such as the following: "The corporation may engage in any activity within the purposes for which a corporation may be organized under this act." [1]
(**3**) The type of corporation. You are asked to check one of three boxes, to indicate if the corporation is (a) a public benefit corporation, organized for a public or charitable purpose; (b) a religious corpora-

---

1   A general purpose clause may be used, as in the case of a corporation organized under the Indiana Business Corporation Law, in other words.

tion, organized exclusively for religious purposes; or (c) a mutual benefit corporation (all others that don't fall into the first two categories).

(4) The post office address of the corporation's initial registered office and the name and address of the corporation's initial registered agent.

(5) Check a box to indicate if the corporation will have members or not.

(6) The name and address of the incorporator(s).

(7) A statement on how the assets of the corporation will be distributed upon dissolution or final liquidation. See the Indiana Code §23-17-22-5 for details on the activities permitted not for profit corporations engaged in winding up and liquidating the corporation's affairs.

At the bottom of the form is space for all the incorporators to sign and print their names and for the person who prepared the form to supply his or her name and address.

So much for filling out the form supplied by the Secretary of State. You can also add additional Articles on a separate sheet or sheets of paper.

In addition to setting forth provisions for managing and regulating the corporation, Articles attached to the form on a separate page may provide that the corporation shall have one or more classes of members, and the qualifications and rights of the members of each class; may limit, enlarge, or deny the right of the members of any class or classes of members, to vote; may extend the right to members to elect the directors of the corporation by cumulative voting procedures (see page 31 for an explanation of cumulative voting); may define, limit, and regulate the rights, powers, and duties of the corporation, its officers, directors, and members; may supersede any provision of the Nonprofit Corporation Act that requires

for approval of corporate action a specific percentage vote of members with any smaller or larger vote requirement; the names and addresses of the persons who will serve as the initial directors.

Names of Not for Profit Corporations

The Secretary of State will not accept any name for a not for profit corporation which implies that the corporation is organized for any purpose other than a purpose for which corporations may be organized under this Act, or a purpose other than the purpose set forth in its Articles of Incorporation. The name of a not for profit corporation *must* contain the word "corporation," "incorporated," "company," or "limited," or an abbreviation of one such word (or similar words or abbreviations in another language). As in the case of profit corporations, the name must be distinguishable from the corporate name of any other domestic or foreign corporation, whether profit or not for profit, already doing business in the state of Indiana.

However, a corporation may take a name that is not distinguishable from the name of another corporation, if at the same time the other corporation changes its corporate name, or dissolves or withdraws from transacting business in this state or ceases to exist. In addition, the other corporation may also give written consent, signed by any current officer of the corporation, to the use of its name by another (in this case, not for profit) corporation.

A not for profit corporation, like a profit corporation, may choose to adopt an assumed corporate name.

The same procedures for reserving a corporate name or checking the availability of a proposed name by telephone, as discussed in Chapter 5, page 53, may be followed. See the Name Reservation form in Appendix E.

Registered Office and Registered Agent

Like a profit corporation, a not for profit corporation must also maintain a registered office (which may be the same as its place of business) and a registered agent. This agent may be anyone who is a resident of Indiana, including, but not limited to, one of the incorporators of the corporation. See the discussion of the registered agent's role in Chapter 5, page 54.

Bylaws

As in the case of a profit corporation, other documents internal to the organization of the corporation, such as the corporate bylaws, are *not* filed with the Secretary of State. After the filing and approval of the Articles by the Secretary of State, the board of directors shall adopt bylaws for the regulation and management of the corporation, covering such issues as the time and place for holding and the manner of conducting meetings; qualifications for membership and its determination; the fees and dues of members; the rights of members; various points concerning the number, qualifications, compensation, and removal of officers and directors and the time, place and manner of electing them; the form of membership certificates; method of changing the bylaws.

Powers of Not for Profit Corporations

The specific authority of not for profit corporations, which enjoy basically the same powers as profit corporations, is spelled out in Section 23-17-4-2 of the Nonprofit Corporation Act.

See the section on "Powers of Profit Corporations" in Chapter 2 (pages 24-25); not for profit corporations possess these same powers.

Membership Book, Minutes, Meeting Notices, Officers' Terms, Quorums, Amendments to Articles, and Dissolution

The not for profit corporation is required to keep a membership book with a record giving the name and address of each member and a financial account of the member's standing. The not for profit corporation is also required to keep correct and complete books of account and the minutes of the proceedings of its members, board of directors, and committees (for rules governing the establishment of committees, see Indiana Code §23-17-15-6). Specific requirements of the Nonprofit Corporation Act also govern such matters as how much advance notice members must be given of meetings of members (not less than 10 days) and meetings of directors (to be prescribed in the bylaws); the minimum number of directors (3); directors' terms of office (a maximum of 5 years); quorums for meetings (a majority unless the Articles or bylaws provide otherwise); amendments to Articles of Incorporation; and voluntary[2] or involuntary[3] dissolution.

Major Differences Between Profit and Not for Profit Corporations

The major differences between a not for profit and a profit corporation in the filing of Articles of Incorporation include the following:

(1) A specific not for profit purpose must be stated in the Articles of Incorporation of a not for profit corporation in order to qualify for nonprofit status with the IRS and the state of Illinois. Be sure that your purpose statement conforms to the requirements of nonprofit status, as defined by the IRS and the state of Illinois.

(2) The corporation must be organized on a nonstock basis.

(3) The filing fee for a not for profit Articles of Incorporation is $30.00.

(4) The not for profit corporation must have a minimum of 3 directors, with the number fixed in the Articles of Incorporation or bylaws.

(5) Unless otherwise provided in the Articles or bylaws, a not for profit corporation must have a president, a secretary, and a treasurer, although an individual may simultaneously hold more than one office.

(6) The not for profit corporation must file an annual report (Indiana Code §23-17-27-8).

Operation under an Assumed Name

As in the case of a profit corporation, a not for profit corporation may also operate under an assumed name, by registering the true and assumed names with the Secretary of State. A copy of the appropriate form is available from the Secretary of State. The fee for registering an assumed name is now $30.

---

2   By decision of the members or the board of directors.
3   In the cases of unpaid taxes, failure to file annual reports, and various other infractions, minor and major—from failure to notify the Secretary of State that the registered agent has been changed to downright abuse of authority and fraud—the corporation may be dissolved by the courts or by the Secretary of State.

Chapter 8. THE S CORPORATION

An S corporation is a special "small business corporation" which has no more than 75 shareholders.[1] This form of operation is normally adopted by relatively small businesses, but larger firms can also elect S status as long as they meet the limitation on the number of shareholders. The 1981 and 1982 tax acts and the Subchapter S Revision Act of 1982 made S corporations easier to form and operate. Consequently, the number of such corporations increased dramatically over the past decade. Some of the tax advantages of S corporations have been reduced under the Clinton tax act. As a result, this form of business operation is no longer as advantageous for certain individuals, particularly ones in the highest tax brackets (36 percent and 39.6 percent).

If a business anticipates large start-up losses in the early years of operation, an S election may be advisable. In the past, *very profitable* businesses also had an advantage when they operated as an S corporation. This was the case because the highest personal tax rate was lower than the highest corporate tax rate, and, as we shall see, the income from S corporations is taxed at the personal tax rate(s) of the owner(s) of the corporation. These two situations, the business with start-up losses and the business that is highly profitable, will be considered in greater depth below.

If you plan to elect S status, consultation with an attorney is recommended, especially with the recent advent of a new type of business entity that is taxed exactly the same way as an S corporation, the limited liability company.

Structure of S Corporations

The S corporation is like a partnership in that it pays no federal taxes in itself. Instead, the income of the corporation is divided in proportion to the stock holdings of the shareholders and is taxed to them as individuals. Likewise, corporate losses are not deducted by the corporation but are passed through directly to the shareholders, who can use the deductions—generally in the year the loss occurs—to offset income from other sources. Like the partnership tax return, the S federal tax return (Form 1120S) is an informational return listing the names of the shareholders and their pro rata share of profits or losses.

---

1   For years, the number of shareholders of an S corporation was limited to 35, but a recent change in the law has upped this figure to 75.

Six Requirements for S Status

A corporation can elect S status by the written consent of all the stockholders, provided it meets six requirements:

1. It must be a domestic corporation (i.e., one located anywhere in the United States).
2. None of the shareholders may be non-resident aliens.
3. There must be no more than 75 shareholders. Shares held in joint ownership by husband and wife (and their estates) are counted as one shareholder.
4. The corporation can't be a member of a group of affiliated corporations (certain corporations which own stock in other corporations are defined by the IRS as "affiliated").
5. There must be only one class of stock, with all shares having equal rights (differences in regard to voting rights *alone* are permitted, however, allowing for voting and non-voting shares, if desired).
6. Banks that use the reserve method of accounting for bad debts, insurance companies subject to tax under the rules of subchapter L, and certain other specialized types of corporations are prohibited from electing S status.

IRS Publication 589 which gave more detailed information concerning S election and other special rules governing S corporations has been inexplicably discontinued. This chapter will cover the main highlights of S election. If more detailed information is required, phone the IRS Taxpayer Assistance line listed in the phone and address directory provided in the back of this book.

Advantage of Voting and Non-Voting Stock

In the past, you were barred from adopting S status if your corporation had both voting and non-voting stock. As pointed out in Chapter 2, the Subchapter S Revision Act of 1982 eliminated this requirement. The creation of non-voting as well as voting stock is now permitted, provided that both voting and non-voting stock are equal in all other respects regarding rights and limitations. This provision makes it very easy to lower taxes by shifting income to family members in lower tax brackets.

By giving non-voting, dividend-paying stock to retired parents or children while keeping voting stock in the hands of the directors of the corporation, you will ease your tax burden without sacrificing control of the company. You do not have to adopt S status in order for your corporation to have both voting and non-voting stock, of course. A regular corporation can have both voting and non-voting stock as well. The point is that S corporations and regular corporations are now on an equal footing in this area, which was not the case in the past.

Applying to the IRS for S Status

Application for S status is made by completing Form 2553. This form is available from the IRS and must be filed at any time on or before the 15th day of the third month of the corporation's tax year or any time during the preceding tax year. For newly formed corporations which wish to begin as

S corporations, this will generally mean filing Form 2553 within 75 days of the date of incorporation. In the event that the IRS later claims non-receipt of the form, it (as well as all other important documents with deadlines) should be sent via certified mail with return receipt requested. This will verify both the mailing and the postmarked date and will stand up in court in the event of any dispute. All the current shareholders of the corporation must agree to the S election, as well as all the persons who were shareholders during the taxable year before the election was made.

Fiscal Year of S Corporations

The fiscal year of newly formed S corporations is now required to be a calendar year (January 1 to December 31) unless there is a business purpose for a fiscal year other than the calendar one.

Revocation of S Status

If stockholders representing a majority of the stock of the corporation file shareholder consents to revocation, S status can be terminated in any successive years. Five years must elapse before you can switch back to S status, however, unless the IRS consents to an earlier re-election. Your S status can also be revoked by the IRS for infringement of the requirements, for instance, if you issue a second class of stock, increase the number of shareholders to more than 75, and so on. Since it may be several years before the IRS discovers that some viola-

tion in the past has voided your S status, a thorough familiarity with the laws governing S corporations is imperative. There are other times when it proves beneficial to a corporation to initiate some action in order deliberately to have its S status revoked.

S Election for Businesses Losing Money

There exist distinct advantages for some individuals in operating an S corporation. If your business is losing money in the first year or two, it may be very beneficial to be able to deduct these losses directly from your personal income on your individual federal income tax return, up to the amount of your basis in the stock of the corporation. In a regular corporation, you have the right to carry these losses forward and deduct them from corporate income in future years when the company is realizing a profit, subject to certain restrictions.

Once the S corporation begins to show a profit, earnings will be taxed at individual shareholder, not corporate, rates. At this point, you may choose to terminate the election and revert to a regular corporation or stay as an S, depending on your individual circumstances. If your corporate tax bracket would be lower than your personal tax bracket, then a regular corporation will be advantageous, from the point of view of taxes. On the other hand, if your personal tax rate is lower than the corporation's would be, an S corporation will allow you to funnel your business income to yourself at lower tax rates. Given the complexity of this issue at present, with the creation of two new personal tax brackets under the Clinton tax act, consultation with a tax adviser is highly recommended if you are considering organizing your business as an S corporation.

S Corporation as Family Tax Shelter

As noted above, S corporations work well as "family tax shelters," since business owners with children or other relatives (on friendly terms!) can issue non-voting, dividend-paying stock to these dependents or relations and keep income within the family at lower personal tax rates. With the Clinton 1993 tax act, the big question now becomes, Will personal tax rates in your individual case be lower than corporate rates, or higher? This is no longer a clear-cut issue for many S corporate owners or potential owners. For the single owner without dependents, a regular corporation may sometimes prove more favorable taxwise these days.

S Format for Profitable Business

In a very profitable business in which dividends have to be issued to escape the IRS's "accumulated earnings penalty," it may very well be advantageous to avoid double taxation on dividends at both the corporate and individual level by opting for S status and paying out all the earnings of the business each year. This tax strategy will work best for small corporations that are profitable, particularly those with large families in which the income can be parceled out among a number of different family members. The windfall dividends may kick you into the highest personal tax bracket. But the tax savings from avoiding double taxation will ordinarily more than offset this disadvantage.

With an S corporation, you are more or less required to distribute all the profits of the corporation within two and one-half months of the end of the tax year or suffer severe tax penalties. Profits not so distributed are considered "constructive dividends" by the IRS and taxed to you individually even though they remain in the corporation.

Obviously, the S arrangement will not work well for capital-intensive businesses which need to accumulate earnings for large capital expenditures on a regular basis, unless the company is prepared to issue bonds or resort to other similar measures to raise needed capital. Generally speaking, a corporation which can pay out virtually all its earnings each year through a combination of deductible expenses (such as salaries, pension plan contributions, and so on) and dividends will function well as an S. For others, there may be potential problems and tax penalties in the case of undistributed income which is "locked in" the S corporation. This is a complicated area, so plan to consult a tax adviser if you are considering forming an S corporation.

Pension Plans of S Corporations; Fringe Benefits

One previous disadvantage of this form of operation was the much smaller pension plan contributions allowable for S corporations, compared to regular corporations. Many of these differences have now been eliminated. On the minus side, the new law makes previously tax-free medical and life insurance benefits taxable to shareholders who own more than 2 percent of the corporation's stock, beginning in 1987. In other words, there is a trade-off. In exchange for the lower tax rates available under certain circumstances to S corporation owners, you lose the opportunity to receive certain tax-free employee fringe benefits.

New Ceiling on Passive Income

The tax law has made S status attractive for certain groups formerly barred from election, such as investment companies and real estate firms and other businesses which typically have large passive income from interest, dividends, annuities, rents, royalties, and gains from sales or exchanges of stock and securities. In the past, S status was denied to companies whose passive income exceeded 20 percent of gross receipts. Since 1983, the ceiling on passive income has been raised from 20 to 25 percent. Even if a company exceeds this limit, its election will not be terminated if the corporation pays a tax of 46 percent of the passive income in excess of 25 percent of gross receipts. Most importantly, any unincorporated business that becomes an S corporation under the new law or any business that has had S status since it originally incorporated can now receive unlimited passive income.

Pass-Throughs in Like Kind

Another major advantage of the new S corporation is that capital gains and tax-exempt income of the company will be passed through to the shareholders in like kind. That is, it will remain taxable at capital gains rates[2] or be tax-free, as the case may be, whereas in the past all such distributions were treated and taxed as ordinary dividend income to the shareholders.

Other Tax Advantages

Several other tax advantages of the S corporation center on the treatment of capital gains and net operating losses. In the past, an owner of a company with a net operating loss exceeding the owner's capital investment could not deduct the amount in excess of the owner's "tax basis." This excess amount can now be carried forward and deducted in future years against corporate profits, provided the owner puts additional capital into the corporation equal to the excess loss deducted. Also,

---

2 At present, the top capital gains tax rate is 28 percent on long-term gains from assets owned more than 12 months

86

shareholders can now report the net operating losses and capital gains of the corporation separately, whereas in the past the two had to be used to offset each other. For S corporations with capital gains and net operating losses, this can mean a substantial tax savings.

Resolutions to Adopt S Status

After weighing the pros and cons, if you choose to organize your business as an S corporation, resolutions to this effect should be included in the Minutes of the First Meeting of the Board of Directors (see Appendix D). For example,

RESOLVED, that the corporation elect to be treated as a "Small Business Corporation" for income tax purposes under Subchapter S of the Internal Revenue Code.

RESOLVED FURTHER, that the officers of this corporation be and hereby are authorized and directed to obtain the written consent of the shareholders to the foregoing election and to file Form 2553 with the IRS.

These two resolutions to adopt S status have, in fact, already been included in the sample Minutes of the First Meeting of the Board of Directors in Appendix D. If you choose *not* to elect S status, these two resolutions should be crossed out.

APPENDIX A

**Articles of Incorporation for Profit Corporations
(Including Professional Service Corporations)**

ARTICLES OF INCORPORATION

State Form 4159 (R10 / 8-95)

Approved by State Board of Accounts 1995

SUE ANNE GILROY
SECRETARY OF STATE
CORPORATIONS DIVISION
302 W. Washington St., **Rm. E018**
Indianapolis, IN 46204
Telephone: (317) 232-6576

INSTRUCTIONS: Use 8 1/2" x 11" white paper for inserts.
Present original and two (2) copies to address in upper right corner of this form.
Please TYPE or PRINT.
Upon completion of filing, the Secretary of State will issue a receipt.

Indiana Code 23-1-21-2
FILING FEE: $90.00

ARTICLES OF INCORPORATION

The undersigned, desiring to form a corporation *(hereinafter referred to as "Corporation")* pursuant to the provisions of:

☐ Indiana Business Corporation Law

As amended, executes the following Articles of Incorporation:

☐ Indiana Professional Corporation Act 1983, Indiana Code 23-1.5-1-1, *et seq.* *(Professional corporations must include Certificate of Registration.)*

ARTICLE I - NAME AND PRINCIPAL OFFICE

Name of Corporation *(the name must include the word "Corporation", "Incorporated", "Limited", "Company" or an abbreviation thereof.)*

Principal Office: The address of the principal office of the Corporation is:

Post office address	City	State	ZIP code

ARTICLE II - REGISTERED OFFICE AND AGENT

Registered Agent: The name and street address of the Corporation's Registered Agent and Registered Office for service of process are:

Name of Registered Agent

Address of Registered Office *(street or building)*	City	Indiana	ZIP code

ARTICLE III - AUTHORIZED SHARES

Number of shares the Corporation is authorized to issue: _____

If there is more than one class of shares, shares with rights and preferences, list such information as "Exhibit A."

ARTICLE IV - INCORPORATORS
[the name(s) and address(es) of the incorporators of the corporation]

NAME	NUMBER AND STREET OR BUILDING	CITY	STATE	ZIP CODE

In Witness Whereof, the undersigned being all the incorporators of said Corporation execute these Articles of Incorporation and verify, subject to penalties of perjury, that the statements contained herein are true,

this _____ day of _____, 19 _____.

Signature	Printed name
Signature	Printed name
Signature	Printed name

This instrument was prepared by: *(name)*

Address *(number, street, city and state)*	ZIP code

APPENDIX B

Bylaws

BYLAWS

of

_____

ARTICLE I
Location

The principal executive office of the corporation in the State of Indiana shall be located in the City/Village/Township of _____ and County of _____. The corporation may have such other offices, either within or without the State of Indiana, as the board of directors may from time to time determine or the business of the corporation may require.

ARTICLE II
Shareholders

Section 1. Place of Meetings. Meetings of the shareholders shall be held at the principal executive office of the corporation or at such other place, within or without the State of Indiana, as the board of directors shall determine.

Section 2. Annual Meeting. The annual meeting of the shareholders shall be held on the ____ day of _____ at _____A.M./P.M. in each year, for the purpose of electing directors and for the transaction of such additional business as necessary. If the day fixed for the annual meeting shall be a legal holiday, the meeting shall be held on the next succeeding business day at the same hour. If the election of directors shall not be held on the day designated herein for any annual meeting, the board of directors shall cause the election to be held at a meeting of the shareholders as soon thereafter as possible.

Section 3. Special Meetings. Special meetings of the shareholders may be called by the president, by the board of directors, or by the holders of at least twenty-five percent of all the outstanding shares of the corporation, upon written demand to the secretary.

Section 4. Notice of Meetings. Written notice stating the place, date, and hour of meetings shall be delivered not less than ten nor more than sixty days before the date of the meeting, either personally or by mail, by or at the direction of the president, or the secretary, or the officer or persons calling the meeting, to each shareholder of record entitled to vote at such meeting. In the case of a special meeting, the purpose or purposes for which the meeting is called shall be included in the notice. In the case of an annual meeting, those matters which the board at the time of the mailing of the notice intends to present for action by the shareholders (but subject to the provision that any proper matter may be presented at the meeting for such action) shall be set forth. If mailed, the notice is given when deposited in the United States mail, with postage thereon prepaid, directed to the shareholder at his address as it appears on the records of the corporation.

Section 5. Meeting of All Shareholders. If all of the shareholders shall meet at any place and time, either within or without the State of Indiana, and consent to the holding of a meeting at such place and time, such meeting shall be valid without call or notice, and at such meeting any corporate action may be taken.

Section 6. Closing of Transfer Books and Fixing of Record Date. For the purpose of determining shareholders entitled to notice of or to vote at any meeting of the shareholders, or shareholders entitled to receive payment of any dividend, or in order to make a determination of shareholders for any other purpose, the board of directors shall provide that the share transfer books be closed for a stated period but not to exceed, in any case, seventy days. If the share transfer books shall be closed for the purpose of determining shareholders entitled to notice of or to vote at a meeting of shareholders, such books shall be closed for at least ten days, or in the case of a merger, consolidation, share exchange, dissolution or sale, lease or exchange of assets, at least twenty days, immediately preceding such meeting. In lieu of closing the share transfer books, the board of directors may fix in advance a date as the record date for any such determination of shareholders, such date in any case to be not more than seventy days and, for a meeting of shareholders, not less than ten days, or in the case of a merger, consolidation, share exchange, dissolution or sale, lease or exchange of assets, not less than twenty days, immediately preceding the meeting. If no record date is fixed for the determination of shareholders entitled to notice of or to vote at a meeting of shareholders, or shareholders entitled to receive payment of a dividend, the date on which notice of the meeting is mailed or the date on which the resolution of the board of directors declaring such dividend is adopted, as the case may be, shall be the record date for such determination of shareholders.

Section 7. Voting Lists. The officer or agent having charge of the transfer books for shares of a corporation shall make, within twenty days after the record date for a meeting of shareholders or five business days before such meeting, whichever is earlier, a complete list of the shareholders entitled to vote at such meeting, arranged in alphabetical order, with the address of and the number of shares held by each, which list, for a period of five business days prior to such meeting, shall be kept on file at the registered office of the corporation and shall be subject to inspection by any shareholder, and to copying at the shareholder's expense, at any time during usual business hours. Such list shall also be produced and kept open at the time and place of the meeting and shall be subject to the inspection of any shareholder during the whole time of the meeting. The original share ledger or transfer book, or a duplicate thereof kept in this State, shall be prima facie evidence as to who are the shareholders entitled to examine such list or share ledger or transfer book or to vote at any meeting of shareholders. Failure to comply with the requirements of this section does not affect the validity of any action taken at such meeting. An officer or agent having charge of the transfer books who shall fail to prepare the list of shareholders, or keep the same on file for a period of five business days, or produce and keep the same open for inspection at the meeting, as provided in this Section, shall be liable to any shareholders suffering damage on account of such failure, to the extent of the damage.

Section 8. Quorum of Shareholders and Voting by Shareholders. Unless a greater or lesser quorum is provided in the Articles of Incorporation, a majority of the outstanding shares, represented in person or by proxy, shall constitute a quorum at a meeting of shareholders, but in no event shall a quorum consist of less than one-third of the outstanding shares. If a quorum is present, the affirmative vote of the majority of the shares represented at the meeting and entitled to vote on a matter shall be the act of the shareholders, unless the vote of a greater number or voting by classes is required by The Business Corporation Law or the Articles of Incorporation. The Articles of Incorporation may require any number or percent greater than a majority up to and including a requirement of unanimity to constitute a quorum.

Section 9. Voting of Shares. Subject to the provisions of Section 12 of this Article, each outstanding share, regardless of class, shall be entitled to one vote upon each matter submitted at a meeting of shareholders, unless the Articles of Incorporation provide otherwise. The Articles of Incorporation may limit or deny voting rights or may provide special voting rights as to any class or classes or series of shares of the corporation.

Section 10. Proxies. At all meetings of shareholders, a shareholder may vote either in person or by proxy executed in writing by the shareholder or by his duly authorized agent or representative. No proxy shall be valid after 11 months from the date of its execution, unless otherwise provided in the proxy.

Section 11. Voting of Shares by Certain Holders. Shares standing in the name of another corporation—domestic or foreign—may be voted by such officer, agent, or proxy as the Bylaws of such corporation may prescribe, or, in the absence of such provision, as the board of directors of such corporation may determine.

Shares of its own stock belonging to this corporation shall not be voted, directly or indirectly, at any meeting and shall not be counted in determining the total number of outstanding shares entitled to vote at any given time, but shares of its own stock held by it in or for an employee benefit plan or in any other fiduciary capacity may be voted and shall be counted in determining the total number of outstanding shares entitled to vote at any given time.

Shares standing in the name of a receiver may be voted by such receiver, and shares held by or under the control of a receiver may be voted by such receiver without the transfer thereof into his name if authority so to do is contained in an appropriate order of the court by which such receiver was appointed.

Shares registered in the name of a deceased person, a minor ward, or a person under legal disability, may be voted by his or her administrator, executor, or court-appointed guardian, either in person or by proxy without a transfer of shares into the name of such administrator, executor, or court-appointed guardian. Shares standing in the name of a trustee may be voted by him or her, either in person or by proxy.

A shareholder whose shares are pledged shall be entitled to vote such shares until the shares have been transferred into the name of the pledgee, and thereafter the pledgee shall be entitled to vote the shares so transferred.

Section 12. Cumulative Voting. If the Articles of Incorporation provide that shareholders in elections for directors shall exercise cumulative voting rights, each shareholder shall have the right to vote, in person or by proxy, the number of shares owned by him or her, for as many persons as there are directors to be elected, or to cumulate said shares, and give one candidate as many votes as the number of directors multiplied by the number of his shares shall equal, or to distribute them on the same principle among as many candidates as he or she shall think fit. A shareholder who has the right to cumulate his or her votes must give written notice to the corporation not less than 48 hours before the time set for the meeting of the shareholder's intent to cumulate the shareholder's votes during the meeting, and if one shareholder gives this notice, all other shareholders in the same voting group participating in the election are entitled to cumulate their votes without giving further notice.

Section 13. Inspectors. At any meeting of shareholders, the chairman of the meeting may, or upon the request of any shareholder shall, appoint one or more persons as inspectors for such meeting.

Such inspectors shall ascertain and report the number of shares represented at the meeting, based upon their determination of the validity and effect of proxies; count all votes and report the results; and do such other acts as are proper to conduct the election and voting with impartiality and fairness to all the shareholders.

Each report of an inspector shall be in writing and signed by him or by a majority of them if there be more than one inspector acting at such meeting. If there is more than one inspector, the report of a majority shall be the report of the inspectors. The report of the inspector or inspectors on the number of shares represented at the meeting and the results of the voting shall be *prima facie* evidence thereof.

Section 14. Action without Meeting. Any action which may be taken at any annual or special meeting of shareholders may be taken without a meeting and without prior notice if a consent in writing setting forth the action so taken shall be signed by the holders of all the outstanding shares entitled to vote or signed by such lesser number of holders as may be provided for in the Articles of Incorporation that would be necessary to authorize or take such action at a meeting.

ARTICLE III
Directors

Section 1. Powers. Subject to any provision in the Articles of Incorporation, including the stipulation that the corporation be run under a shareholders' agreement, the business and affairs of the corporation shall be managed by a board of directors.

Section 2. Number. The authorized number of directors shall be _____ until changed by amendment to this Article of these Bylaws.

Section 3. Election and Term of Directors. Each director shall hold office until the next annual meeting of shareholders or until his successor shall have been elected and qualified, or until his prior resignation or removal. Unless otherwise provided in the Articles of Incorporation, a director may be removed, with or without cause, by vote of the holders of a majority of the shares entitled to vote at an election of directors, subject to the Business Corporation Law. A director may be removed by the shareholders only at a meeting called for the purpose of removing the director and the meeting notice must state that the purpose, or one of the purposes, of the meeting is removal of the director. Directors need not be of a set age, residents of Indiana, or shareholders of the corporation unless the Articles of Incorporation so prescribe.

Section 4. Vacancies. Any vacancy occurring in the board of directors and any directorship to be filled by reason of an increase in the number of directors may be filled by election at an annual meeting or at a special meeting of sharcholders called for that purpose. A director elected to fill a vacancy shall serve until the next annual meeting of shareholders at which directors are to be elected.

Section 5. Regular Meetings. A regular meeting of the board of directors shall be held without other notice than this Bylaw, immediately after and at the same place as the annual meeting of shareholders. The board of directors may provide, by resolution, the time and place, for the holding of additional regular meetings without other notice than this resolution.

Section 6. Manner of Convening Special Meetings. Special meetings of the board of directors may be called by or at the request of the president or any two directors.

Section 7. Place of Special Meetings. The person or persons authorized to convene special meetings of the board of directors may fix any place, either within or without the State of Indiana, as the place for holding any special meeting of the board of directors.

Section 8. Notice of Directors' Meetings. Special meetings of the board of directors shall be held upon at least two days' prior notice in writing, delivered personally or mailed to the business address of each director. Any director may waive notice of any meeting. Attendance of a director at any meeting shall constitute a waiver of notice of such meeting except where a director attends a meeting for the express purpose of objecting to the transaction of any business because the meeting is not lawfully called or convened. Neither the business to be transacted at nor the purpose of any regular or special meeting of the board of directors need be specified in the notice or waiver of notice of such meeting.

Section 9. Quorum of Directors. A majority of the number of directors fixed by the Bylaws shall constitute a quorum for the transaction of business. The act of the majority of the directors present at a meeting at which a quorum is present shall be the act of the board of directors.

Section 10. Informal Action by Directors. Unless specifically prohibited by the Articles of Incorporation, any action required to be taken at a meeting of the board of directors may be taken without a meeting if a consent in writing, setting forth the action so taken, shall be signed by all the directors entitled to vote.

Section 11. Dissent. A director of a corporation who is present at a meeting of its board of directors at which action on any corporate matter is taken is conclusively presumed to have assented to the action taken unless his dissent is entered into the minutes of the meeting or unless he files his written dissent to such action with the person acting as the secretary of the meeting before the adjournment thereof or forwards such dissent by registered mail to the secretary of the corporation immediately after the adjournment of the meeting. Such right to dissent does not apply to a director who voted in favor of such action.

Section 12. Compensation. By the affirmative vote of a majority of directors, the board shall have authority to establish reasonable compensation for all directors in payment for actual services to the corporation as directors, officers, or otherwise. A fixed sum and expenses for actual attendance at each regular or special meeting of the board may also be authorized.

ARTICLE IV
Officers

Section 1. Number. The officers of the corporation shall be a president, a vice-president, a secretary and a treasurer, as well as other additional officers whose titles and duties shall be determined by the board of directors. Any two or more offices may be held by the same person. The corporation must have at least one officer.

Section 2. Election. An officer of the corporation shall be chosen by the board of directors. Each officer shall hold office until his death, resignation or removal as hereinafter provided. A vacancy in any office because of death, resignation or removal or other cause shall be filled by the board at either an annual or special meeting.

Section 3. Resignation and Removal. An officer may resign at any time upon written notice to the corporation. An officer may be removed at any time, either with or without cause, by the board, but such removal shall be without prejudice to the contract rights, if any, of the person so removed.

Section 4. President. The president shall be the chief executive officer of the corporation, and, subject to the direction and control of the board of directors, shall manage the business of the corporation and shall see that all orders and resolutions of the board are carried out. He or she shall preside at all meetings of the shareholders and directors and shall have such other powers and duties as may from time to time be prescribed by the board of directors or Bylaws.

Section 5. Vice-President. During the absence or disability of the president, the vice-president, or, if there are more than one, the executive vice-president, shall possess all powers and functions of the president. Any vice-president may sign, with the secretary, certificates for shares of the corporation, and shall perform such other duties as may from time to time be prescribed by the board of directors or the Bylaws.

Section 6. Secretary. The secretary shall keep or cause to be kept, at the principal executive office of the corporation, the minutes of all meetings of the shareholders and of the board of directors. The secretary shall see that all notices of meetings are given in accordance with the provisions of these Bylaws or as required by law. The secretary shall have charge of the corporate seal and shall affix it to any instrument when authorized by the board of directors. The secretary shall keep or cause to be kept, at the principal executive office of the corporation or at the office of the corporation's transfer agent, a share register, showing the names of the shareholders and their addresses, the number and classes of shares held by each, the number and date of certificates issued for shares, and the number and date of cancellation of every certificate surrendered for cancellation. The secretary shall keep or cause to be kept, at the principal executive office of the corporation, the original or a copy of the Bylaws and amendments, the resolutions of the shareholders, and other documents of the corporation, and shall certify that all such documents of the corporation are true and correct copies. The secretary shall perform whatever other duties as may be prescribed by the board.

Section 7. Treasurer. The treasurer shall have charge of the corporate funds and securities; shall keep or cause to be kept complete and accurate account books of corporate receipts and payments; deposit all money and other valuables in the name of the corporation in such banks, trust companies or other depositories as designated by the board of directors; prepare and present financial reports to the annual meeting of shareholders and the regular meetings of the board of directors, and perform such other duties as are assigned to him or her from time to time by the board of directors.

Section 8. Sureties and Bonds. If required by the board of directors, any officer of the corporation shall give to the corporation a bond for the faithful performance of his or her duties in such sum and with such surety or sureties as the board shall determine.

Section 9. Compensation. The salaries of the officers shall be fixed from time to time by the board of directors. No officer shall be prevented from receiving such salary due to the fact that he or she is also a director of the corporation.

ARTICLE V
Certificates for Shares

Section 1. Certificates. The shares of the corporation shall be represented by certificates. The form of such certificates shall be determined by the board of directors, in accordance with the requirements of the Indiana Business Corporation Law. All certificates shall be numbered and entered in the books of the corporation upon issue. They shall show the holder's name and the number of shares and shall be signed by two officers of the corporation (or the sole officer, if the corporation has only one officer), and shall bear the corporate seal. In addition, they shall state that the corporation is formed under the laws of the state of Indiana and shall indicate (1) the class of shares (if there is more than one) and (2) the designation of the series (if any). In the case of a lost or destroyed certificate, an affidavit of the fact shall be made by the person claiming the certificate to be lost or destroyed. The board may direct a new certificate to be issued as a replacement for that one alleged to be lost or stolen and may, at its discretion, require a bond as indemnity against any claims that may arise regarding the certificate alleged lost or stolen.

Section 2. Transfer of Shares. All certificates surrendered to the corporation by the holder of record or his authorized representative shall be cancelled and a new certificate issued to the transferee. All such transfers shall be entered in the transfer book of the corporation, kept at its principal executive office or the office of its transfer agent. No transfer shall be made within ten days preceding the annual meeting of shareholders. The holder of record of any share shall be regarded as the holder in fact for all purposes as regards the corporation.

ARTICLE VI
Waiver of Notice

Any notice required to be given under the provisions of these Bylaws, the Articles of Incorporation, or the provisions of The Business Corporation Law may be waived by the individual entitled to such notice. A waiver in writing signed by said individual, whether before or after the time stated in the notice, shall be deemed equivalent to the giving of such notice.

ARTICLE VII
Dividends

The board of directors may declare and the corporation may pay dividends on its outstanding shares from time to time, subject to the provisions of The Business Corporation Law and the corporation's Articles of Incorporation: No dividends shall be declared or paid at a time when the corporation is insolvent or its net assets are less than zero, or when the payment thereof would render the corporation insolvent or reduce its net assets below zero. Directors who authorize dividends when dividends are not permitted to be paid (under the Indiana Statutes, section 3-1-28-3) are held personally liable for their actions.

ARTICLE VIII
Amendment of Bylaws

Bylaws may be adopted, altered, amended, or repealed at any meeting of the board of directors of the corporation by a majority vote of the directors present at the meeting.

CERTIFICATE

This is to certify that the foregoing is a true and correct copy of the Bylaws of the corporation named in the title thereto and that such Bylaws were duly adopted by the board of directors of said corporation on the date set forth below.

DATED:

_____
Secretary

(seal)

APPENDIX C

**Waiver of Notice
Minutes of First Meeting of Shareholders**

WAIVER OF NOTICE AND CONSENT TO HOLDING OF FIRST MEETING OF SHAREHOLDERS

of

_____

We, the undersigned, being all the shareholders of _____, an Indiana corporation, hereby waive notice of the first meeting of the shareholders of the Corporation and consent to the holding of said meeting at _____ in _____, Indiana, on _____, 19 ____, at _____A.M./P.M., and consent to the transaction of any and all business by the Shareholders at the meeting, including, without limitation, the approval of the Articles of Incorporation, the recording of the Certificate of Incorporation, the approval of the preorganization subscription agreement (if applicable), and the election of directors.

DATED:

_____
Shareholder

_____
Shareholder

_____
Shareholder

_____
Shareholder

_____
Shareholder

_____
Shareholder

MINUTES OF FIRST MEETING OF SHAREHOLDERS
OF

_____

The Shareholders of _____ held its first meeting on
_____, 19 _____ at _____ A.M./P.M. at _____ in
_____, Indiana. Written waiver of notice was signed by all the Shareholders and attached
to the minutes of this meeting.

        The following Shareholders, being the owners of a majority of the outstanding shares and
constituting a quorum, were present at the meeting:

_____

_____

_____

_____

_____

_____

These were represented by proxy:

_____

_____

_____

These were absent:

_____

_____

_____

        On motion and by unanimous vote, _____ was elected temporary
Chairman and presided over the meeting. _____ was elected temporary Secretary
of the meeting.

        The Chairman advised that the Articles of Incorporation had been filed and a Certificate of
Incorporation issued by the Indiana Secretary of State. Upon the presentation of these documents to the meeting, a
motion was duly made, seconded and unanimously carried that the Articles of Incorporation be approved and the
Certificate recorded.

        The Chairman presented to the meeting the preorganization subscription agreement (if applicable)
of the Corporation. It was read and formally approved by the Shareholders.

        By unanimous vote, the following persons were elected Directors, to hold office until the next
annual meeting of Shareholders, and until the election and qualification of their successors:

NAME   ADDRESS

_____   _____

_____   _____

_____   _____

_____   _____

_____   _____

        Since there was no further business to come before the meeting, on motion duly made and seconded,
the meeting was adjourned.

DATED:

_____
                Secretary

The following are appended hereto:
        WAIVER OF NOTICE OF MEETING
        COPY OF CERTIFICATE OF INCORPORATION
        PREORGANIZATION SUBSCRIPTION AGREEMENT (if applicable)

APPENDIX D

Waiver of Notice
Minutes of First Meeting of Board of Directors

WAIVER OF NOTICE AND CONSENT TO HOLDING OF FIRST MEETING OF BOARD OF DIRECTORS
OF
_____

We, the undersigned, being all the directors of _____, an Indiana corporation, hereby waive notice of the first meeting of the board of directors of the corporation and consent to the holding of said meeting at _____ in _____, Indiana, on _____, 19 _____, at _____A.M./P.M., and consent to the transaction of any and all business by the directors at the meeting, including, without limitation, the adoption of Bylaws, the election of officers, the adoption of the corporate seal and stock certificates, the establishment of the corporation's fiscal year, and the selection of a bank or banks where the corporation will maintain accounts.

DATED:

_____
Director

_____
Director

_____
Director

_____
Director

MINUTES OF FIRST MEETING OF BOARD OF DIRECTORS
OF

_____

The first meeting of the board of directors was held at _____ _____ in _____, Indiana, on _____, 19_____, at _____ A.M./P.M. The following directors, constituting a quorum of all the directors of the corporation, were present.

_____

_____

_____

_____

_____ was nominated and by unanimous vote elected temporary chairman, and presided over the meeting until relieved by the president.

_____ was nominated and elected by unanimous vote as temporary secretary, and acted as such until relieved by the permanent secretary. The secretary then presented to the meeting the Waiver of Notice of Meeting signed by all the directors, and upon a motion duly made, seconded, and carried, the waiver was appended to the minutes of the meeting.

The chairman then presented to the meeting a certified copy of the Articles of Incorporation which had been filed with the Indiana Secretary of State on _____, 19 _____. The secretary was instructed to append the copy to the minutes of the meeting.

The chairman thereupon presented to the meeting a copy of the proposed bylaws of the corporation. After consideration and discussion, it was unanimously

RESOLVED, that the corporation adopt as the bylaws of this corporation the bylaws presented to this meeting.

The following persons were nominated and unanimously elected officers of the corporation to serve for one year and until their successors are elected and qualified:

_____ President
_____ Vice-President
_____ Secretary
_____ Treasurer

The president thereafter presided at the meeting and the permanent secretary replaced the temporary secretary.

Upon motion duly made, seconded, and carried, it was

RESOLVED, that the form of the corporate seal presented at the meeting, an impression of which is directed to be made by the secretary in the margin of these minutes, be and hereby is adopted as the seal of this corporation.

Upon motion duly made, seconded, and carried, it was further

RESOLVED, that the form of stock certificate submitted to this meeting be and hereby is adopted for the issuance of share certificates by the president and secretary. A copy of the stock certificate so adopted is to be attached to these minutes, and further

RESOLVED, that the principal executive office of this corporation shall be at _____ in _____, Indiana.

Upon motion duly made, seconded, and carried, it was

RESOLVED, that the fiscal year of this corporation shall end on the _____ day of the month of _____ of each year.

Upon motion duly made, seconded, and carried, it was

RESOLVED, that the treasurer be and hereby is authorized to open a bank account with _____ located at _____ and a resolution for that purpose on the printed form of said bank(s) was adopted and instructed to be attached to these minutes.

Upon motion duly made, seconded, and carried, it was

RESOLVED, that the Medical Reimbursement Plan presented to this meeting be and hereby is adopted as the medical reimbursement plan of the corporation.

Upon motion duly made, seconded, and carried, it was

RESOLVED, that the following annual salaries be paid to the officers of this corporation:
PRESIDENT;
VICE-PRESIDENT:
SECRETARY:
TREASURER:

Upon motion duly made, seconded, and carried, it was

RESOLVED, that the corporation elect to be treated as a "Small Business Corporation" for income tax purposes under Subchapter S of the Internal Revenue Code.

RESOLVED FURTHER, that the officers of this corporation be and hereby are authorized and directed to obtain the written consent of the shareholders to the foregoing election and to file Form 2553 with the IRS.

RESOLVED, that the officers of the corporation be authorized to sell and issue shares of stock in exchange for money and property, not to exceed $1,000,000 in amount, and further

RESOLVED, that this sale and the organizing and managing of the corporation shall be carried out as a "Small Business Corporation," to the end that any shareholder who experiences a loss on the transfer of shares of common stock of the corporation may qualify for an "ordinary" loss deduction on his personal income tax return.
Upon motion duly made, seconded, and carried, it was

RESOLVED, that whereas the Articles of Incorporation authorize the issuance of _____ shares of capital stock, this corporation shall sell an aggregate of not to exceed _____ shares of its capital stock at a purchase price of $_____ per share, in consideration of money paid to the corporation, as follows:

Name(s) of Purchaser(s)	Number of Shares	Amount of Money

RESOLVED FURTHER, that this corporation sell and issue an aggregate of not to exceed _____ shares of its capital stock at a purchase price of $_____ per share, upon delivery of said assets to the corporation, as follows:

Name(s) of Purchaser(s)	Number of Shares	Description of Property

Upon motion duly made, seconded, and carried, it was

RESOLVED, that the corporation accept the written offer dated _____, 19 _____, to transfer the assets and liabilities of said business, in accordance with the terms of said offer, a copy of which is attached to the minutes of this meeting.

RESOLVED FURTHER, that the board of directors hereby determine that the fair market value of said business to the corporation is $_____.

Since there was no further business to come before the meeting, on motion duly made, seconded, and carried, the meeting was adjourned.

DATED:

_____
Secretary

The following are appended hereto:
WAIVER OF NOTICE OF MEETING
CERTIFIED COPY OF ARTICLES OF INCORPORATION
SAMPLE STOCK CERTIFICATE
BANK DEPOSITORY RESOLUTION FORM
MEDICAL REIMBURSEMENT PLAN (if applicable)
OFFER OF TRANSFER OF BUSINESS (if applicable)

APPENDIX E

Name Reservation Application
Preorganization Subscription Agreement
Incorporation Under a Close Corporation Agreement
Bill of Sale Agreement
Medical and Dental Reimbursement Plan
Articles of Incorporation for Not for Profit Corporations

APPLICATION FOR RESERVATION
OF EXCLUSIVE USE OF CORPORATE NAME
State Form 26233 (R / 1-88)
Approved by the State Board of Accounts, 1988

Provided by

Sue Anne Gilroy
Secretary of State
Corporations Division
302 W. Washington St. Rm. E018
Indianapolis, IN 46204
Telephone: (317) 232-6576

Indiana Code 23-1-23-2

FILING FEE $20.00

Instructions: Present original and one copy to the address in the upper
                       right corner of this form.

Proposed Name to be reserved:
Name of applicant:
Address of applicant   Zip Code
Signature   Printed Name

FOR USE BY SECRETARY OF STATE OFFICE ONLY

☐   The name is available and reserved for 120 days from the date stamped on this application.

☐   The name is indistinguishable from a name on the records of the Secretary of State and is therefore

      unavailable.

NOTE: The owner of the reserved name may transfer the reservation to another person by delivery to the Secretary of

              State of signed notice of the transfer. The notice must state the name and address of the transferee and the

              original approval date or have an attached copy of the original file - marked application for reservation of a corporate name.

PREORGANIZATION SUBSCRIPTION AGREEMENT

We, the undersigned, severally subscribe to the number of shares set opposite our respective names of capital stock of a proposed corporation, to be known as _____ or by any other name that the incorporators may select, and to be incorporated in the State of Indiana. We agree to pay the sum of $_____ per each share subscribed.

This subscription shall not be binding on the undersigned unless subscriptions in the aggregate amount of $_____ for shares of said corporation have been procured on or before the _____ day of _____, 19 _____.

All subscriptions hereto shall be payable at such time or times as the board of directors of said corporation may determine and shall be paid in cash, except as hereinafter indicated. (If any of the subscriptions are to be paid by transferring property to the corporation, a description of the property shall be attached hereto.)

Date _____ Name and Address _____ Number of Shares _____ Amount Subscribed

INCORPORATION UNDER A CLOSE CORPORATION AGREEMENT

RESTRICTIONS ON TRANSFER OF SHARES

The Articles of Incorporation may list one or more restrictions on the transfer of issued shares of stock. The stock certificates of your close corporation must either spell out the restriction(s) on the certificates themselves or state, on the face or back of the certificates, that a statement detailing the restriction(s) shall be furnished by the corporation to any sharcholder upon request and without charge.

The following types of restrictions may be listed in the Articles of Incorporation.

RIGHT OF FIRST REFUSAL. This kind of restriction requires a shareholder to offer to the corporation or to one or more shareholders of the corporation or to any other designated person or to any combination of the above a prior opportunity to acquire his or her shares.
PRIOR CONSENT. This kind of restriction obligates the corporation or the holders of shares of any class of the corporation to consent to any proposed transferee of the shares.
SUBCHAPTER S TRANSFERS. This type of restriction prohibits a transfer of shares if such would cause the corporation to lose its elected status as a "small business corporation" under Subchapter S of the Internal Revenue Code.
PROHIBITED TRANSFERS. This type of restriction forbids a transfer of shares to designated persons or classes of persons, provided such a prohibition is not manifestly unreasonable.
OTHERS. Any other lawful restriction on transfer of shares may be made in the Articles of Incorporation.

MANAGEMENT OF CORPORATION BY SHAREHOLDERS

The Articles of Incorporation of a close corporation may provide that the business of the corporation shall be managed by the shareholders of the corporation rather than by a board of directors. So long as this provision continues in effect, (1) No meeting of shareholders need be called to elect directors; (2) Unless the context clearly requires otherwise, the shareholders of the corporation shall be deemed to be directors for purposes of applying provisions of the Indiana Business Corporation Law, as now or hereafter amended; (3) The shareholders of the corporation shall be subject to all liabilities of directors.

BILL OF SALE AGREEMENT

The corporation, _____, and the business owner(s)
_____, hereafter called the "transferor(s)," enter into the following
agreement:

      1. In return for the issuance and delivery of _____ shares of stock of _____
_____, an Indiana corporation, I (we) hereby sell, assign, and transfer to the corporation all my (our) right,
title, and interest in the following property:
      a. All the tangible assets listed on the inventory attached to this Bill of Sale, and all stock in trade,
trade, goodwill, trade names, trademarks, service marks, leasehold interests, copyrights and other intangible assets
(excluding—list any non-transferred assets:) of
_____, located at _____ Street,
_____,
_____ County, Indiana.
      2. In return for the transfer of the above property to it, the corporation hereby agrees to assume, pay,
and discharge all debts, duties, and obligations that appear on the date of this agreement, on the books and owed on
account of said business (excluding—list any unassumed liabilities:).
The corporation agrees to indemnify and hold the transferor(s) of said business and their property free from any
liability for any such debt, duty, or obligation and from any suits, actions, or legal proceedings brought to enforce or
collect any such debt, duty, or obligation.
      3. The transferor(s) hereby appoint(s) the corporation as his (her, their) representative to demand,
receive, and collect for itself, all debts and obligations now owing to said business (excluding—list any unassumed
debts:). The transferor(s)
further authorize(s) the corporation to do all things allowed by law to recover and collect such debts and obligations
and to use the transferor's (s') name(s) in such manner as it considers necessary for the collection and recovery of
such debts and obligations, provided, however, without cost, expense, or damage to the transferor(s).

DATED:

_____
(Transferor)

_____
(Transferor)

_____
(Transferor)

_____
(Name of Corporation)
By: _____
          (Title)

_____
          (Title)

MEDICAL AND DENTAL CARE REIMBURSEMENT PLAN
OF

_____

1. BENEFITS

The corporation shall reimburse all eligible employees for expenses incurred by themselves and their dependents, as defined in IRC S152, as amended, for medical care, as defined in IRC S213(e), as amended, subject to the conditions and limitations as hereinafter set forth. It is the intention of the Corporation that the benefits payable to eligible employees hereunder shall be excluded from their gross income pursuant to IRC S105, as amended.

2. ELIGIBILITY

All corporate officers employed on a full-time basis at the date of inception of this Plan, including those who may be absent due to illness or injury on said date, are eligible employees under the Plan. A corporate officer shall be considered employed on a full-time basis if said officer customarily works at least seven months in each year and twenty hours in each week. Any person hereafter becoming an officer of the Corporation, employed on a full-time basis, shall be eligible under this Plan.

3. LIMITATIONS

(a) The Corporation shall reimburse any eligible employee without limitation/no more than $_____ (cross out one) in any fiscal year for medical care expenses.

(b) Reimbursement or payment provided under this Plan shall be made by the Corporation only in the event and to the extent that such reimbursement or payment is not provided under any insurance policy(ies), whether owned by the Corporation or the employee, or under any other health and accident or wage continuation plan. In the event that there is such an insurance policy or plan in effect, providing for reimbursement in whole or in part, then to the extent of the coverage under such policy or plan, the Corporation shall be relieved of any and all liability hereunder.

4. SUBMISSION OF PROOF

Any eligible employee applying for reimbursement under this Plan shall submit to the Corporation, at least quarterly, all bills for medical care, including premium notices for accident or health insurance, for verification by the Corporation prior to payment. Failure to comply herewith may, at the discretion of the Corporation, terminate such eligible employee's rights to said reimbursement.

5. DISCONTINUATION

This Plan shall be subject to termination at any time by vote of the board of directors of the Corporation; provided, however, that medical care expenses incurred prior to such termination shall be reimbursed or paid in accordance with the terms of this Plan.

6. DETERMINATION

The president shall determine all questions arising from the administration and interpretation of the Plan except where reimbursement is claimed by the president. In such case, determination shall be made by the board of directors.

ARTICLES OF INCORPORATION

State Form 4162 (R8 / 6-95) Corporate Form No. 364-1 (October 1984)
Approved by State Board of Accounts 1995

SUE ANNE GILROY
SECRETARY OF STATE
CORPORATIONS DIVISION
302 W. Washington St., **Rm. E018**
Indianapolis, IN 46204
Telephone: (317) 232-6576

INSTRUCTIONS: Use 8 1/2" x 11" white paper for inserts.
Present original and two (2) copies to address in upper right corner of this form.
Please TYPE or PRINT.
Upon completion of filing the Secretary of State will issue a receipt.

Indiana Code 23-17-3-2
FILING FEE: $30.00

* For tax exempt status, Nonprofit Corporations must qualify with both the Internal Revenue Service and the Indiana Department of Revenue.

ARTICLES OF INCORPORATION

The undersigned incorporator or incorporators, desiring to form a corporation *(hereinafter referred to as the "Corporation")* pursuant to the provisions of the Indiana Nonprofit Corporation Act of 1991 *(hereinafter referred to as the "Act")*, execute the following Articles of Incorporation.

ARTICLE I - Name and Principal Office

Name of the Corporation: *(the name must include the word "Corporation", "Incorporated", "Limited", "Company" or one of the abbreviations thereof):*

Principal Office: The address of the principal office of the Corporation is:

Street office address	City	Indiana	ZIP code

ARTICLE II - Purpose *(optional)*

The purposes for which the Corporation is formed are:

ARTICLE III - Type of Corporation *(check only one)*

The Corporation is a:

☐ public benefit corporation, which is organized for a public or charitable purpose;

☐ religious corporation, which is organized primarily or exclusively for religious purposes; or

☐ mutual benefit corporation *(all others).*

ARTICLE IV - Registered Agent and Registered Office

Registered Agent: The name and street address of the Corporation's Registered Agent and Registered Office for service of process are:

Name of Registered Agent

Address of Registered Office *(street or building)*	City	Indiana	ZIP code

ARTICLE V - Membership

Indicate if Corporation will have members:

☐ Yes   ☐ No

(Continued on the reverse side)

ARTICLE VI - Incorporator(s)

Name(s) and address(es) of the incorporator(s) is/are as follows:

Name	Number and Street or Building	City	State	ZIP code

ARTICLE VII - Distribution of Assets on Dissolution or Final Liquidation

Refer to Indiana Code 23-17-22-5 for permitted activities following Dissolution.

THIS DOCUMENT MUST BE SIGNED BY ALL INCORPORATORS.

I (we) hereby verify, subject to penalties of perjury, that the facts contained herein are true. *(Notorization not necessary)*

Signature	Printed name
Signature	Printed name
Signature	Printed name

This instrument was prepared by: (*name*)

Address	City	State	ZIP code

Incorporation Checklist

Action	Pages where discussed	Completed
1. Select your corporate name (*Read* Naming Your Business and Its Products and Services; *Contact The P. Gaines Co. for trade name and trademark searches*)	*51-53*	
2. Prepare your Articles of Incorporation	*53-59*	
3. File your Articles of Incorporation	*59*	
4. Apply for corporate Employer Identification Number	*70-71*	
5. Notify creditors (in the case of incorporating a going business)	*60*	
6. Order the Corporate Records Book and Seal	*61*	
7. Prepare the Preorganization Subscription Agreement (if applicable)	*62-63*	
8. Prepare the Bylaws	*64*	
9. Prepare the Minutes of the First Meeting	*64-68*	
10. Issue shares of stock	*68-70*	
11. File Assumed Name Report (if applicable)	*71*	

IMPORTANT ADDRESSES AND PHONE NUMBERS

INDIANA SECRETARY OF STATE
Corporation Division
302 West Washington Street
Room E 018
Indianapolis, Indiana 46204
Telephone (317) 232-6576

CORPORATE INFORMATION LINES

Preliminary name check for
availability of corporate names

Telephone (317) 232-6576

Legal section—general information on
filing Articles of Incorporation, fees, status
of filing; may also provide limited assistance in
handling certain types of complaints against
corporations for alleged violations of
various corporations statutes (cannot handle
consumer complaints against corporations)

Telephone (317) 232-6581

Forms request
Corporate forms by fax

Telephone (317) 232-6576
Telephone 1-800-726-8000

Certifications section—prepares certified
copies of documents, certificates of existence,
due and diligent searches, and specified certificates
certifying other information on file in the Corporations
Division Office

Telphone (317) 232-6584

Biennial reports information

Telephone (317) 232-6596

Trademarks information

Telephone (317) 232-6681

SECURITIES DIVISION
302 West Washington Street
Room E 111
Indianapolis, Indiana 46204
Telephone (317) 232-6681

DEPARTMENT OF REVENUE
Form order 24-hour hotline (317) 486-5103
Sales tax telephone (317) 233-4015
Corporation tax section telephone (317) 232-2189

Withholding tax section telephone (317) 233-4016
Sales tax registration telephone (317) 232-2240
Not-for-profit section telephone (317) 232-2188

DEPARTMENT OF EMPLOYMENT AND TRAINING SERVICES
Before hiring employees, apply for an unemployment compensation number:
Telephone (317) 232-7436

WORKERS' COMPENSATION

In Indiana, you must set up Workers Compensation through a private insurance company.
Regarding Workers' Compensation disputes, contact:
Telephone (317) 232-3809

INTERNAL REVENUE SERVICE

To request that IRS forms and publications be mailed to you, call tollfree: **1-800-TAX-FORM**

To receive federal tax information by phone, call tollfree: **1-800-829-1040**

ZONING AND LICENSING

*Be sure to contact the county clerk and
the city clerk in the area in which you
live in regard to zoning and any licenses
or permits required to conduct business
in their jurisdiction.*

Index

Small Business Bookshelf Series
Volume 2 (ISBN 0-936284-10-2)   **$19.95**

NAMING YOUR BUSINESS AND ITS PRODUCTS AND SERVICES: How To Create Effective Trade Names, Trademarks, and Service Marks To Attract Customers, Protect Your Good Will And Reputation, And Stay Out Of Court

Every business, no matter how small, needs a company trade name. In addition, manufacturers and companies providing services to the public may require distinctive names for their goods (trademarks) and services (service marks). This book explains the crucial differences between these three types of names used in commerce, the name selection process, and the legal cautions and pitfalls.

Topics covered include:
• The difference between trademarks, copyrights, and patents
• What determines ownership of a trademark or service mark
• Why trade names are *not* registrable with the Patent and Trademark Office (PTO)
• Why *all* trade names, whether used by sole proprietors, partnerships, or corporations, should be "cleared" for possible infringements of other trade names, trademarks, and service marks
• Why existing businesses that failed to research their trade names for possible legal violations before going into business should do so *now*, instead of later
• Why clearance of a name by the Corporation Division of a given state offers no guarantee of trademark or trade name clearance
• How to do computer and manual trademark and trade name searches, including the use of the TRADEMARKSCAN® data base, Shepard's *Citations,* and industry and trade directories
• How what you don't know *can* hurt you in the realm of trademark law
• The main differences between state and federal trademark laws
• The 8 advantages of federal trademark registration
• The federal trademark registration process; the differences between the Principal Register and the Secondary Register
• Why family surnames are disallowed as registrable trademarks or service marks by the PTO, with one exception
• The risks and rewards of names that parody or satirize, such as LARDASHE® jeans for overweight people
• Why you do *not* have to register your trademark or service mark with the PTO in order to use the symbol™
• Why you *must* register your trademark or service mark with the PTO to use the symbol ®
• Why a term that is "merely descriptive" of a company's goods or services, such as "Lite" (for a type of beer) or "Super glue"(for a type of super-adhesive) cannot be registered as a trademark
• The use of symbols, puns, and historical, mythical, and literary allusions as effective marks
• Name-coining techniques

The P. Gaines Co. now offers computer trademark and service mark searches and company name searches. **Both types of seach include**: (1) a computer search of Dun and Bradstreet's Electronic Business Directory, a listing of some 9 million U.S. businesses; (2) a computer search of TRADEMARKSCAN®, scanning both the currently active state and federal trademark registrations in <u>all</u> classes; (3) a computer search of TRADE NAME DATABASE, consisting of trade names and common law trademarks (not registered) as well as registered trademarks compiled by Gale Research in <u>Brands and Their Companies</u>.; (4) a search of some 20 additional data bases where business names appear is also included. Check the order form for additional information.

THE BLACK BEAUTY CORPORATE KIT
(See Order Blank on Next Page)

The Black Beauty Corporate Outfit

By special arrangement with Julius Blumberg, Inc., The P. Gaines Co. will provide a complete corporate kit with the following outstanding features:

1. A three-ring Corporate Record Book with 24K gold trim and lustrous black vinyl slip case. Corporate name is printed on a gold label and inserted into acetate label holder. Record Book includes a Stock Transfer Ledger of 8 pages, bound in a separate section, Mylar-coated Index Tabs, with five important divisions, 50 blank sheets of rag content 20-lb. bond Minute Paper, and exclusive Corporate Record Tickler.

2. A Corporate Seal stored inside the Corporate Record Book in a zipper pouch, 1 5/8" diameter, custom finished with corporate name, state, and year. Long corporate names (over 45 characters and spaces) require a 2" diameter seal, at an extra charge of $8.00.

3. 20 custom printed and numbered Stock Certificates with full page numbered stubs. Each certificate is custom printed with corporate name, state, and member titles.

ORDER FORM—Remit with payment to The P. Gaines Co., Box 2253, Oak Park, IL 60303

For all corporate kit orders, please type or print the following information:

Corporate name exactly as on certificate of incorporation...
State of incorporation..
Year of incorporation..
Officers who will sign share certificates (President and Secretary-Treasurer will be listed unless specified otherwise)..

Basic price of corporate kit	$69.95
For long corporate names	
(over 45 characters and spaces), add an additional $8.00	_.__
7.75% Illinois sales tax (Illinois residents only)	5.42

Choose **one** of the following two modes of shipping and cross out the other:

Shipping by UPS (delivery within 2 weeks from receipt of your order)	4.00
OR Shipping by Air Express (delivery within 4 days from receipt of order)	25.00

(*4-day Air Express orders must be paid for with Certified Check, Money Order, or credit card)

TOTAL _____

Ship to:

Your name..Address..Phone.................

(Street address required)

City..State...Zip...............................

Charge to my: _____Visa _____Mastercard
Card#:_____Expires:_____

Exact name on credit card_____

Signature_____

For faster service, call in your credit call order at 1-800-578-3853. Total cost of the Black Beauty Corporate Outfit, with regular shipping via UPS, is $73.95.

Order Form

Remit check or M.O. with order to The P. Gaines Co., PO Box 2253, Oak Park, Illinois 60303

Credit Card Orders: Mail in order (supply information below) or call tollfree: 1-800-578-3853

Title	Cost	Number of copies	Total
How to Form Your Own Michigan LLC* (*Limited Liability Company) Before the Ink Dries!	$26.95		
Small Time Operator	$14.95		
Five Easy Steps to Setting Up a Retirement Plan	$14.95		
The Partnership Book	$26.95		
Starting and Operating a Business in Indiana	$24.95		
Naming Your Business and Its Products & Services	$19.95		
Pennsylvania Incorporation Manual (1st ed)	$24.95		
Illinois Incorporation Manual, With Disk (5th ed)	$31.95		
Michigan Incorporation Manual (2nd ed)	$24.95		
Ohio Incorporation Manual (2nd ed)	$24.95		
Indiana Incorporation Manual, With Disk (2nd ed)	$31.95		
Missouri Incorporation Manual (1st ed)	$19.95		
Minnesota Incorporation Manual (1st ed)	$24.95		
How to Write a Business Plan	$21.95		
Clearing Your Business Name (Computer search)	$95.00		

Check one: ☐ Company Trade Name Search

Name of Company: _____

Main Business Activity: _____

Or ☐ Trademark or Service Mark Search

Name of product or service: _____

Type of goods or services:_____

Subtotal			
7.75% sales tax (Illinois residents only)			
Shipping ($3.50 for first book; $1.00 for each additional title)			
GRAND TOTAL (please enclose check , M.O., or credit card information)			

Name..

Address...Phone..............................

Charge to my: _____Visa _____Mastercard
Card#:_____Expires:_____

Exact name on credit card_____

Signature:_____